THE SOUL OF SOIL

THE SOUL OF SOIL

*A Soil-Building Guide
for Master Gardeners
and Farmers*

FOURTH EDITION

Grace Gershuny and Joe Smillie

CHELSEA GREEN PUBLISHING
White River Junction, Vermont

Designed by Dede Cummings Designs

Printed in the United States
Fourth edition. First Chelsea Green printing, 1999

19 18 17   8 9 10

Library of Congress Cataloging-in-Publication Data

Gershuny, Grace.
    The soul of soil : a soil-building guide for master gardeners and
farmers / Grace Gershuny and Joe Smillie. —4th ed.
        p.   cm.
    Includes bibliographical references.
    ISBN 1-890132-31-4 (alk. Paper)
    1. Soil management.   2. Organic farming.   3. Agricultural
ecology.
I. Smillie, Joseph. II. Title.
S591.G45   1999
631.4—dc2   99-20865
                                                CIP

Chelsea Green Publishing
85 North Main Street, Suite 120
White River Junction, Vermont 05001
(802) 295-6300
www.chelseagreen.com

*This work is dedicated
to life on earth
and all soil lovers.*

CONTENTS

List of Tables

FOREWORD TO THE FOURTH EDITION

What a joy it is
to feel the soft, springy earth under my feet
   once more,
to follow grassy roads that lead to ferny brooks
where I can bathe my fingers in a cataract of rippling notes,
or to clamber over a stone wall into green fields that
tumble and roll and climb in riotous gladness!

—HELEN KELLER, from *The Story of My Life*

Cultivating soil and encouraging plants to grow in harmony with nature's wondrous systems has been an honored avocation throughout history. But modern Western society, with all its advances, sometimes brings a disconnection from our Earth. I believe we are in a period of reawakening, making a transition from a mechanical to a biological era. Our knowledge and our actions in all fields, from human health to forestry and agriculture, will be built on a combination of knowledge about biological systems and acceptance of our own role in nature.

Feeling this connectedness to our planet and the living systems around us will be one of the predominant experiences of the twenty-first century. These experiences will not all be joyous. Some will be more painful than the DDT death of eagles or the phosphate and nitrate poisoning of our waterways. The changes we are making to nature's balanced systems are leading to a cascade of environmental problems. To our credit, we are beginning to reverse the damage to the air-water-soil-plant-animal systems, as demonstrated by the cleanup of rivers in North America.

The first rule of ecology is that everything is connected to everything else, and so when any one component changes, everything else changes in response, even if only a tiny bit. Getting in touch with the "soul of soil" is a crucial first step toward honoring our oneness with all living creatures and helping the long process of repair that a new biological era will require.

Joe Smillie and Grace Gershuny are uniquely qualified to write this book, which I consider to be the most clear and concise introduction to the magic of how soil works. This is also an ideal guide to how one can respect soil and be gentle and aware when working with it. The authors combine university training with practical field experience and decades of successful results. Joe has probably visited and helped more organic farmers around the world than anyone else I know. Grace teaches organic agriculture, farms organically, and has committed her life to the soil. She too has spent many years inspecting and helping organic farms around the world.

At the root of successful farming and gardening is the principle that a healthy soil yields bountiful plants resistant to disease and insect pests. This knowledge is not new. It has been observed and proven by practical farmers and agricultural experts for centuries. Thomas Jefferson, in a 1793 letter to advising his daughter about pest problems, wrote:

> When the Earth is rich, it bids defiance to droughts, yields in abundance, and of the best quality. I suspect that the insects which have harassed you have been encouraged by the feebleness of your plants, and that has been produced by the lean state of your soil.

More recently, Sir Albert Howard, one of the founding fathers of organic farming, linked quick-fix synthetic nitrogen fertilizers to increased pest problems:

> Nature has provided a marvelous piece of machinery for conferring disease resistance on the crop. This machinery is only active in soil rich in humus; it is inactive or absent in infertile land and in similar soils manured with chemicals. The fuel needed to keep this machinery in motion is a regular supply of freshly prepared humus, properly made. Fertile soils then yield crops resistant to disease. Worn-out soils, even when stimulated with chemical fertilizers, result in produce which needs the assistance of insecticides and fungicides to yield a crop at all [from *An Agricultural Testament*].

One of the great myths of the twentieth century held that *organic farmers have fewer tools at their disposal. They can't compete or succeed on a large scale.* And yet ecological or organic soil care is actually built around what R. Buckminster Fuller called "doing more with less." Thus we reduce inputs by encouraging air in the soil, letting earthworms be our plowmen and fertilizer factories, and growing legumes to collect nitrogen for free from the air thanks to that extraordinary symbiotic relationship between good bacteria and certain plant roots. These are among the wondrous insights you can glean from The Soul of Soil, and these are the tools that land stewards of every persuasion will need for us all to thrive in the twenty-first century. As Wendell Berry has written, in *The Gift of Good Land*:

> An organic farm, properly speaking, is not one that uses certain methods and substances and avoids others; it is a farm whose structure is formed in imitation of the structure of a natural system that has the integrity, the independence, and the benign dependence of an organism.

The thin mantle of "soul" that covers our Earth is what feeds and nurtures us. We are innately and inextricably connected to soil for our survival. Yet today we are paving over this life-giving, breathing mantle and washing countless billions of tons of soil into our waterways, as though it were just dirt. What if we had to take into consideration what an earthworm would really like? It would certainly change how we do environmental impact studies!

For twenty years, my work in organic soil care and ecological earth management has joyously led me to cross paths with Grace and Joe. I remember reading the manuscript for the first edition and knowing that this primer outlines the essential dynamics of the living soil. Here is the working person's introduction to agronomy, because it provides the basic information you need to become a self-educated soil expert. In a reader-friendly way, *The Soul of Soil* also lays out the basic tenets of a sustainable agriculture.

With this knowledge you too can know the joy of helping your soils improve. Observing your soil, counting your earthworms, measuring drainage, feeling texture, smelling the forest earth smell, and knowing what these indicators mean will empower you to be a steward of the soil and the bounty it yields. Learning a few simple tests that you can do at home connects you directly to nature's systems. In fact, it's more important to learn those simple tests than to learn how to take a soil sample and send it off to a lab. Having provided the fundamentals, Joe and Grace go on to explain all about taking and interpreting laboratory soil tests.

There is a strong spiritual bond between humans and the other living souls with whom we share this planet. In today's fast-paced world, the music of that bond sometimes gets lost. Soil, like humans, has soul because it contains the universal life-force. This is the difference between soil and dirt — life energy. The diverse and amazing creatures of the soul, from earthworms to fungi — the "microflora people" — provide the energy that drives our food system, including all of the land plants that cleanse our air and produce our oxygen, and all of the land plants that we eat and feed to our animals.

I give thanks for this energizing spring of life beneath my feet. Have you ever noticed the difference in your spirit and body, between walking on concrete and walking on springy, living, healthy soil? I hope you too will enjoy connecting with *The Soul of Soil.*

BILL WOLF
Past President, Organic Trade Association (OTA)
Founder and Past President, Necessary Trading Company
Founding President, Organic Materials Review Institute (OMRI)

ACKNOWLEDGMENTS

This book was first published in 1983 by the Extension Service of the University of Vermont, having been undertaken by Grace Gershuny as part of a Masters program in Extension Education. Joe Smillie, originally a reviewer and mentor of this work, significantly expanded and improved the original in 1986, resulting in a self-published second edition that received widespread attention. This fruitful collaboration continued, despite increasingly busy work schedules and life changes, when agAccess published a revised and expanded third edition in 1994. We are now pleased to be working with Chelsea Green to bring out an updated fourth edition of *The Soul of Soil*. Many people have helped us at different stages of drafting, publishing, and revision. The list has grown too long to mention everyone, but credit should be given to the early support and technical expertise lent by Bart Hall, Robert Parnes, Will Brinton, Win Way, and Bill Liebhardt. Stuart Hill and his associates at the Ecological Agriculture Project in Canada were an invaluable source of information, and Fred Franklin challenged us to stay on the cutting edge. Fred Magdoff, Miranda Smith, and Bill Wolf are among the early reviewers who have continued to give good counsel about matters technical and philosophical as we have expanded our knowledge of both soil and life. Grace developed parts of the third edition in the course of writing a book for home gardeners entitled *Start with the Soil*, published by Rodale Press in 1993. In addition, we would like to thank Ben Watson of Chelsea Green for his skillful editing of the present edition.

Our best advisors have been the many organic farmers we have been privileged to visit, work, play, and live with. Friends and colleagues of NOFA (Northeast Organic Farming Association) and the Organic Trade Association, as well as the many similar groups around the nation and the world, have offered continual inspiration. The experience of working for USDA has confirmed Grace's belief in the fundamental importance of soil to everything we do. This understanding was shared by her colleagues, Michael Hankin and Ted Rogers, whose friendship and good humor made it possible to keep going with a thankless task. Her associates at the Institute for Social Ecology in Plainfield, Vermont, along with her students at Goddard College, have kept that awareness alive in countless ways. Joe would like to acknowledge his colleagues at OTA, especially members of the Quality Assurance Council and executive director Katherine Dimatteo. His sources of inspiration were the soil microbes and earthworms of Erle, and organic farmers Paul Keene, Rajah Bannerjee, Dave Riebling, Paul Buxman, Denzil Sosa, Alan Derting, and the market gardeners of China.

Both of us owe much to the personal, moral and creative support of our families. Stewart Hoyt, Grace's ex-husband, did most of the illustrations for the earlier editions. Susan Boyer, Joe's wife, produced the second edition. Friends in Jamaica, especially current spouse Bentley Morgan, helped Grace gain new perspectives and learn a little about tropical agriculture. Our children, Opal Hoyt and Megan, Adrienne and Ellen Smillie are who it's all for.

THE SOUL OF SOIL

INTRODUCTION

There are as many different concepts of farming as there are farmers. The past fifty years have witnessed the rapid industrialization of agriculture, with spectacular improvements in yields per acre and per person-hour. But these achievements have come at a high social and environmental cost, leading to widespread doubt about the wisdom of treating agriculture as just another industrial process. Today, biotechnologists are attempting to speed up this revolution even more; if the ultimate scenario of industrial agriculture is the farmerless farm, that of biotechnology could well be the farmless food system.

The farm crisis of the eighties has not disappeared. Farms are still getting fewer and larger overall, while chronic problems of "surplus" and low prices plague those farmers who hold on. Global market forces are subjecting small farmers everywhere to the whims of giant commodity traders. Topsoil in the Corn Belt is eroding faster than during the Dust Bowl days of the thirties, and ecological destruction threatens farmland throughout the Third World and former Soviet bloc. Farmworkers worldwide face serious health problems from exposure to pesticides—many banned in the U.S.—while pests grow increasingly resistant.

Early critics of industrialized agriculture, such as Sir Albert Howard and J.I. Rodale, used the term "organic" to describe farming methods based on living processes. That word has stuck, especially in the minds of consumers, who now demand "organically grown" foods when they are looking for products grown without synthetic pesticides in an ecologically sound manner. "Biological" is also a popular term, especially in Europe, and avoids the confusion caused by those who point out that all carbon-based compounds—including pesticides, herbicides, and other petroleum products—are technically defined as "organic." Some like to refer to "regenerative" agriculture to emphasize the need to repair some of the ecological damage done to soil and water.

In recent years, many of these concepts have become accepted within the established agricultural research and educational institutions. In fact, "sustainable" agriculture, once a nearly interchangeable term with "organic," has become the new mandate for many federal and state agricultural programs in the U.S. and worldwide. The 1992 United Nations Earth Summit, in fact, established sustainable agriculture as one of the key areas of emphasis in order to reverse the planet's current course toward ecological destruction. Yet the term "sustainable" eludes easy definition and stands for a set of general principles rather than as a marketplace label. "Low-input," referring to reduced reliance on off-farm inputs, has also been used to characterize alternative agriculture in a way that emphasizes the economic benefit of decreased production costs.

While we have worked with constituencies who identify with all of these different terms, the one we prefer is "ecological" agriculture or "agro-ecology." The science of ecology emphasizes the interrelations between all living things and their environment, which includes social, economic, and political relationships. As this understanding takes root on more working farms, it will come to be known simply as "good farming": that which is based on resource-efficient and ecologically harmonious methods.

Whichever terminology feels most comfortable to you, soil management is the basis of farm productivity, and therefore the cornerstone of any ecologically sound approach to farming. The most crucial element in any plan for conversion is the soil management plan. Many other farm decisions, including crop selection and equipment purchases, must be made with consideration of soil management needs. And once you have grasped the complex dynamics of the soil ecosystem, you will more easily perceive other practical applications for agro-ecological principles. While reliance on purchased inputs is reduced, increased skill, observation, and management capabilities are required in order to eliminate the need for the fast-acting remedies relied on in conventional systems.

There is continuing controversy about what methods and materials constitute ecological or sustainable agriculture, but there are now fairly specific regulatory stipulations about practices permitted for organic farming. While we have participated in many of these discussions, this book is not intended as a set of authoritative prescriptions. Rather, we hope it will be used as a reference and an aid to planning, adapted to the unique needs of the reader. More information related to requirements for organic certification is found in chapter 5, and occasional comments are included throughout the text as to the acceptability, according to legal definitions of organic, of various materials and practices under discussion.

It is often difficult for those wishing to practice ecological methods to find information and advice about how to do it. Traditional sources such as Extension and farm suppliers, although they have made considerable progress in recent years, are still limited by their lack of practical knowledge, their limited budgets, and their conflicting desire for increased sales. Nonprofit nongovernmental organizations are generally underfunded and poorly staffed, often lacking basic agricultural knowledge. Much can be learned from other farmers, trial and error, and diligent research, but there is a real need for practical guidelines to help make sound soil management decisions based on ecological principles. That is the purpose of this book.

This book was originally written from a northeastern U.S. bioregional perspective. This edition has been considerably revised to reflect our wider experience in other regions of this country and the world, and to make the information more directly applicable in other places. The principles of ecological soil management can be used by farmers anywhere to improve the health of their soil and the productivity of their farm operations.

BASIC DEFINITIONS AND TENETS OF ECOLOGICAL FARMING

USDA: Principles of Organic Production Systems

These principles were derived from various definitions used by organic producer groups, and formed the bases for drafting the National Organic Program proposed rule published in December, 1997.

Organic production systems seek to provide food, fiber, and herbal products of the highest quality in sufficient quantities. The following principles are the foundation of organic management methods:

1. Protect the environment, minimize pollution, promote health, and optimize biological productivity.
2. Replenish and maintain long-term soil fertility by providing optimal conditions for soil biological activity.
3. Maintain diversity within the farming system and its surroundings and protect and develop plant and wildlife habitat.
4. Recycle materials and resources to the greatest extent possible within the farm and its surrounding community as part of a regionally organized agricultural system.
5. Provide attentive care that meets both health and behavioral requirements of farm animals.

6. Maintain the integrity and nutritional value of organic food and processed products through each step of the process from planting to consumption.
7. Develop and adopt new technologies with consideration for their long-range social and ecological impact.

~&~

The Organic Trade Association

The Organic Trade Association (OTA), formerly the Organic Foods Production Association of North America (OFPANA), has developed Guidelines for Certification Organizations, *which include the following definitions:*

Organic foods are produced under a system of ecological soil management that relies on building humus levels through crop rotations, recycling organic wastes, and applying balanced mineral amendments. This, along with the use of resistant varieties, minimizes disease and pest problems. When necessary, mechanical, botanical, or biological controls with minimum impact on health and environment may be used. Organic foods are processed, packaged, transported, and stored to retain maximum nutritional value without the use of artificial preservatives, coloring, or other additives, irradiation, or synthetic pesticides.

Sustainable agricultural systems are based on ecological soil management practices that replenish and maintain soil fertility by providing optimum conditions for soil biological activity. They aim to reduce the use of off-farm inputs, environmental and health hazards associated with agricultural chemicals, and reliance on nonrenewable resources. Sustainable agricultural systems are modeled on natural ecosystems in which diversity, complexity, and recycling of energy and nutrients are essential.

Earth Summit Alternative Nongovernmental Sustainable Agriculture Treaty

Sustainable agriculture is a model of social and economic organization based on an equitable and participatory vision of development that recognizes the environment and natural resources as the foundation of economic activity. Agriculture is sustained when it is ecologically sound, economically viable, socially just, culturally appropriate, and based on a holistic scientific approach . . . Sustainable agriculture respects the ecological principles of diversity and interdependence and uses the insights of modern science to improve rather than displace the traditional wisdom accumulated over centuries by innumerable farmers around the world.

UNDERSTANDING THE SOIL ECOSYSTEM

The first step toward effective ecological soil management is an appreciation of the complex, living system known as soil. And to understand soil is to be aware of how everything affects and is affected by it. We are all part of the soil ecosystem.

Soil fertility can be described as its capacity to nurture healthy plants. Sustainable agriculture aims to protect the soil's ability to regenerate nutrients lost when crops are harvested—without dependence on "off-farm" fertilizers. This regenerative capacity, in turn, depends on the diversity, health, and vitality of the organisms that live, grow, reproduce, and die in the soil. Through the activities of soil microbes—which can number in the billions in every gram of healthy topsoil—the basic raw materials needed by plants are made available at the right time, and in the right form and amount.

The basic aim of ecological soil management is to provide hospitable conditions for life within the soil.

Your farm is both the product and producer of soil. Consider your farm to be a living organism that achieves its greatest long-term productivity when its natural cycles and processes are enhanced. Shortcutting these cycles for short-term control or economic gain will eventually bear out the ecological maxim, "The creature that wins against its environment destroys itself."

The place to start is where you are. Thousands of soil types have been named, classified, and described. Knowing their names can tell you a lot about their general characteristics; but, like any living creature, each individual is unique. Find out what soils live in your area, how they are classified and described by soil scientists, and how that compares with what you observe about them yourself.

Soil classification schemes organize soils according to their different qualities, based on the kinds of minerals they contain, how they were formed, and various physical characteristics. The individual character of any soil arises from a combination of factors inherent to its particular geographic region (see table 1).

Table 1

ENVIRONMENTAL INFLUENCES ON SOIL

Climate. Temperature and precipitation affect the rate of organic matter accumulation and the presence of soluble soil minerals. For example, more organic matter accumulates where decomposition is slow due to cooler temperatures, while high rainfall leaches mineral nutrients from topsoil.

Native vegetation. Grasslands, forests, and transition zones each affect soil development in a different way. Leaf litter from pine forests, for example, increases soil acidity. Soil particles developed under grasslands are usually bound into stable aggregates by the activity of the plentiful microorganisms and roots found there.

Parent material. Underlying rock types from which it was formed determine a soil's mineral content and basic textural qualities. Limestone bedrock, for instance, helps counteract soil acidity. Red soils indicate that the parent material and derived soil is rich in iron. Volcanic ash eventually produces soils heavy in amorphous clays.

Topography. Soil may be eroded from slopes and deposited in lowlands. The legendary fertility of river valleys such as the Nile resulted from deposits of rich sediment carried from the highlands, while mountain farmers all over the world have problems holding onto precious topsoil.

Time. The availability of minerals and the extent of humus development in soil is also influenced by how long the native rock has been subject to weathering. Young soils, such as those in Hawaii and other areas of volcanic activity, may be low in clay, which is produced by the chemical effects of weathering on parent rocks.

Glaciation and geologic activity. In the north-temperate region, the advance and retreat of glaciers, most recently a mere 12,000 years ago, has had a significant effect on soil formation and quality. Volcanic activity has left nutrient-rich lava deposits in many areas.

Soils worldwide have been classified into ten major orders (see table 2). In humid temperate regions such as the northeastern United States, where forests are the predominant natural vegetation, the soil order of **spodosols** is most common. These soils are generally formed from coarse-textured parent material, and tend to be quite acidic and low in mineral nutrients. Prairie soils, which have developed under flat, grass-covered areas with modest rainfall, are classified as **mollisols**. They are among the most naturally productive soils, with high native organic matter and mineral content. In tropical regions with very high seasonal rainfalls, the heavily leached **ultisol** soils also tend to acidity. The Sahara, Gobi, and Turkestan Deserts, as well as South and Central Australia and the American Southwest are largely comprised of **aridisols**. If irrigated they can be productive, but great care must be taken to prevent toxic accumulations of soluble salts.

Each order is further broken down into suborders, great groups, and subgroups. Beyond this, soils are described in terms of families, associations, and series, which provide more information about their plant growth characteristics, organic and mineral content, structure, drainage, and color. Series are often named after the places—towns, rivers, or counties—where they are located.

Your local Extension or Soil Conservation Service office can probably give you a soil map for your land. They can also show you your county's soil survey, which provides detailed information on local soils and their best uses, as well as helpful climatological data.

Table 2
THE TEN MAJOR SOIL ORDERS

Entisols: Recently formed mineral soils with little evidence of horizon formation. Found in a wide range of climate zones, including the Rocky Mountains, the Sahara Desert, Siberia, and Tibet. May be highly productive, but most are relatively barren.

Vertisols: Mineral soils with a high content of swelling-type clays, which in dry seasons cause the soils to develop deep cracks. Found in some areas of the southern U.S., India, Sudan, and eastern Australia. Their physical properties make them difficult to till and cultivate.

Inceptisols: Young soils with limited horizon formation. May be very productive, as those formed from volcanic ash. Found in the Pacific Northwest (U.S.), along the Amazon and Ganges Rivers, North Africa, and eastern China.

Aridisols: Mineral soils found mostly in dry climates. Productive only if irrigated, and may become saline. Found in the southwestern U.S., Africa, Australia, and the Middle East.

Mollisols: Characterized by a thick, dark surface horizon, they are among the world's most productive soils, with high natural fertility and tilth. Generally found under prairie vegetation, such as the Great Plains (U.S.), Ukraine, parts of Mongolia, northern China, and southern Latin America.

Spodosols: Mineral soils characterized by distinct horizons, including subsurface organic matter, and aluminum and sometimes iron oxides. Coarse-textured, readily leached, and tending to be acid, they occur mostly in humid, cold temperate climates, generally under forests. Can be very productive if properly fertilized.

Alfisols: Moist mineral soils with high base status and presence of silicate clays. Found mostly in humid regions under deciduous forest or grass including parts of the U.S. Midwest, northern Europe, southern Africa, and Southeast Asia. Highly productive, good nutrient levels and texture.

Ultisols: Moist soils that develop under warm to tropical climates. Highly weathered, acidic, with red or yellow subsurface horizons. Found in the humid southeastern U.S., Southeast Asia, and southern Brazil. Can be highly productive, with good workability.

Oxisols: The most highly weathered soils, with a deep subsurface horizon of iron and aluminum oxides. High in clay, commonly deficient in phosphosurfaces. Not well adapted to mechanized farming, they have been poorly researched.

Histosols: Organic soils that have developed in a water-saturated environment, with at least 20 percent organic content. Can be very productive if drained, especially for vegetable crops.

SOURCE: adapted from Nyle Brady, *The Nature and Properties of Soils*, 10th ed.

ORGANIC MATTER AND HUMUS

Soil health and **humus** are indivisible: health is the vitality of the soil's living population, and humus is the manifestation of its activities. As the cornerstone of the soil ecosystem, humus influences and is influenced by every other aspect of the soil. Building soil humus improves its physical and chemical properties as well as its biological health.

All humus is organic matter, but not all organic matter is humus. Raw organic matter consists of the waste products or remains of organisms that have not yet decomposed. Humus is one form of organic matter that has undergone some degree of decomposition. There is no hard and fast dividing line, but a continuum, with fresh, undecomposed organic materials—manure, sawdust, corn stubble, kitchen wastes, or insect bodies—at one end, and stable humus, which may resist decomposition for hundreds of years, at the other. Table 3 summarizes the attributes of different types of organic matter and humus.

Humus is dark brown, porous, spongy and somewhat gummy, and has a pleasant earthy fragrance. Chemically, it is a mixture of complex compounds, some of which are plant residues that don't readily decompose, such as waxes and lignins. The rest are gums and starches synthesized by soil organisms, primarily bacteria and fungi, as they consume organic debris. Humus is highly variable in its composition, depending on the nature of the original material and the conditions of its decomposition.

"Humus" is actually more a generic term than a precise one. Its qualities will reflect different origins and composition. Just as wine can vary widely in quality, so can humus. And, just as different wines are suitable for different culinary purposes, the varieties of humus serve varying soil functions.

Several classification schemes for humus have been suggested. Theories differ as to how it is formed, why it behaves as it does, and how it should be measured. Humus that can still decompose readily is known as effective or active humus. It consists of a high proportion of simple organic acids (fulvic acids), which will dissolve in either acids or bases. This type of humus is an excellent source of plant nutrients, released as soil organisms break it down further, but of little consequence for soil structure and long-term tilth. This kind of humus is mainly derived from the sugar, starch, and protein fraction of organic matter.

Humic acids, which dissolve in bases but not in acids, characterize more stable or passive humus; humins, which are highly insoluble and may be so tightly bound to clay particles that microbes can't penetrate them, are the main constituents of the most stable humus. Because stable humus resists decomposition it does little to add nutrients to the soil system, but it is essential to improving the soil's physical qualities. Carbon-14 dating has revealed that very stable humus complexes may survive unchanged for thousands of years. Stable humus originates from woodier plant residues, which contain lots of cellulose and lignin.

The status of soil organic matter and humus is a dynamic one, continually changing through the activities of all the creatures that live there. Ideally, there should be a rough equilibrium among the different kinds of humus at any one time, with the more active fractions predominant when plant nutrient needs are highest, then giving way to more stable forms after harvest or when plants are dormant. Fungi and actinomycetes, which are more abundant than bacterial decomposers under cool, damp conditions, are also more important in the creation of stable humus.

The changes are fastest under optimum conditions for soil biological activity, and fresh supplies of raw organic matter must continually be added to keep the cycles moving. Anything that harms or disrupts one member of the soil community can lead to a form of "indigestion" in the soil. For example, if large amounts of nitrate fertilizer flood the soil system, the bacteria responsible for converting protein fragments into nitrates will be suppressed, in turn "backing up" the whole organic decomposition process. They will recover after a while, but if this process is repeated year after year, the capacity of that soil to digest fresh organic matter will be seriously damaged.

The process by which organic matter and humus breaks down in the soil is called **mineralization**. While humus is the product of organic matter mineralization, it too can be mineralized under the right conditions. Organic matter management, discussed in chapter 3, requires that you understand what conditions speed up or slow down mineralization.

Mineralization occurs quickly when conditions are perfect for bacteria to reproduce: high aeration, adequate moisture, good pH, and balanced mineral nutrients. Cultivation speeds it up by introducing air; if soil is dry, irrigation will also stimulate mineralization. Increasing soil temperature with dark mulch or row covers, or actually heating the soil in a greenhouse bed, also encourages the faster release of nutrients to plants.

As is true with fertilizing, it's important to understand the concept of "enough" when you choose to stimulate mineralization. Too quick a release of nutrients from organic matter can cause problems, which parallel those of overfertilizing: excess plant nitrate uptake or possible leaching of nutrients into groundwater. It's also important to avoid "burning up" vital, stable humus reserves by making sure to add enough organic matter to replenish what is mineralized.

Humus tends to accumulate fastest under conditions unfavorable to mineralization: cool temperatures, low pH, and poor aeration. While to some extent this is desirable, the extreme example of going too far is the case of a peat bog, composed of almost pure humus. The key here is balance: an active, healthy biological population will continually be mineralizing humus at the same time that it is being formed. As you become attuned to the signs of biological activity and health in your soil, as well as the rhythms of growth and rest in your crops, you will develop a better sense of "enough" when it comes to humus formation and decay.

BENEFITS OF HUMUS

- Humus can hold the equivalent of 80 to 90 percent of its weight in water, so soil rich in humus is more drought-resistant.
- Humus is light and fluffy, allowing air to circulate easily, and making soil easy to work.
- The sticky gums secreted by microbes while forming humus hold soil particles together in a desirable crumb structure.
- Humus is extremely effective at holding mineral nutrients safe from being washed away in rain or irrigation water, and in a form readily available to plants. Ample reserves of humus also provide additional plant nutrients in times of need.
- Humus is able, because of its biochemical structure, to moderate excessive acid or alkaline conditions in the soil—a quality known as buffering.
- Many toxic heavy metals can be immobilized by soil humus, and prevented from becoming available to plants or other soil organisms.
- Although the color of humus can vary, it is usually a dark brown or black color, which helps warm up cold soils quickly in the spring.

Table 3

THE NATURE AND FUNCTION OF ORGANIC MATTER AND HUMUS

	Raw organic matter	*Effective humus*	*Stable humus*
		NATURE	
Source	Wastes, residues, and remains of living organisms.	Decomposed raw organic matter.	Decomposed raw organic matter or effective humus.
Composition	Complex organic compounds, such as proteins, cellulose, lignins, fats, starches and sugars.	Characterized by high ratio of fulvic acids (small, soluble molecules).	Mostly long-chained humic acids, or humins bonded to clay particles.
Characteristics	Heterogeneous, coarse, lumpy material.	A colloid, more homogeneous in texture and color.	Homogeneous, resistant to chemical action.
		FUNCTION	
Physical	Improves aeration, drainage, and moisture retention. "Trash mulch" protects soil from weathering. If too coarse and abundant, may hinder seed preparation.	Creates "crumb structure"—spongy, porous, and sticky—that makes an excellent soil conditioner. Dark brown color improves heat retention by soil.	Same as effective humus.
Chemical	Provides some soluble nutrients, especially from manures. Leaves a reserve supply of nutrients in the soil. Releases much carbon dioxide as it decomposes.	Mobile in soil; readily releases nutrients to plants. Holds nutrient anions in a form available to plants, but safe from leaching. Increases cation exchange capacity.	Provides long-term nutrient storage and maintains good cation exchange capacity. Toxic substances (as well as nutrients) can be chelated and prevented from entering the ecosystem.
Biological	Provides food for microbial decomposers. However, if too carbonaceous, can overstimulate microbes and lock up available nitrates.	Provides nutrients to microbes as it decomposes. Releases vitamins, hormones, antibiotics, and other biotic substances.	Provides microbial habitat and evidence of healthy biological activity.

PHYSICAL FACTORS: SOIL STRUCTURE AND TILTH

Tilth is to soil what health is to people. A soil in good tilth is in good physical condition for supporting soil life. Good tilth also means soil is loose and easy to work, so tools as well as plant roots can readily dig in. Moisture and aeration are the key physical qualities of soil. The ability of soil to hold water without becoming soggy, and to allow air to penetrate to plant roots and other soil organisms, is vital to every aspect of fertility.

The tilth of your soil is a composite of its texture, structure, aggregation, density, drainage, and water-holding capacity. No matter what kind of soil you start out with, most of these qualities can be improved by increasing its organic matter and humus content.

Soil Composition

About half the volume of a good, loamy soil is pore space—the area between particles where air and water can penetrate. The pore space is generally an equal volume of air and water, which clings to the surface of soil particles. Don't discount the importance of pore spaces. All the fertilizer in the world won't solve the problems created by dense, compacted soil that is deficient in pore space.

FIGURE 1. *Soil particles and pore spaces, showing a thin film of water covering each particle.*
(Drawing by Timothy Rice.)

Of the solid half of the soil, about 90 percent is composed of small bits of the rocks and minerals from which the soil was formed, as well as clays created by the weathering of the parent rock. The remaining 10 percent is the organic fraction. The influence of this small part of the soil on its ability to support plant growth is tremendous.

The sand and clay components of a soil are largely unalterable—there's not much you can do to change them. But how you manage your soil can have a profound influence on the amount and quality of organic matter it contains. The organic fraction of the soil is a dynamic substance, constantly undergoing change. It consists of living organisms, including plant roots and bacteria, as well as dead plant residues and other wastes. The total weight of the living organisms in the top six inches of an acre of soil can range from 5,000 to as much as 20,000 pounds.

Fundamental Qualities

Every soil has its own unique physical characteristics, which are determined by how it was formed. Some of these qualities can be improved with proper management—or made worse by abuse—but others must simply be considered the basic starting point you must work with. There's not much you can feasibly do to change the depth of bedrock or water table, or to eliminate a steep slope. You can pick rocks out of a very stony soil, but in cold climates, frost-heaving will only bring more rocks to the surface each spring.

Soil texture is one such inherent quality. Texture can range from very fine, mostly clay particles, to coarse and gravelly ones. Any extreme is undesirable: the ideal loamy texture is a balance of fine clay and silt, combined with coarse sand. The texture of your soil will influence its nutrient status, workability, aeration, and drainage. Clay soils hold water and nutrients well, but can be poorly drained and difficult to work. When they dry out, they form hard clumps, and can take on the consistency of concrete. Sandy soils are generally easy to work and well drained, but have poor nutrient- and water-holding ability. Their very high aeration means organic matter decomposes too rapidly, and little stable humus is formed.(Refer to chapter 3 for instructions on evaluating your soil's texture and other physical qualities.)

Structure and Aggregation

Good tilth is less dependent on the composition of your soil than on how it holds together. The ability of soil particles to form stable aggregates, giving it a crumbly, cake-like consistency, determines its structural soundness. The ideal crumb structure, illustrated below, is very much a product of biological activity. Humus plays a central role in forming soil aggregates, but many soil creatures—most notably earthworms—secrete the sticky gums that are crucial for holding soil particles together. Structure and aggregation can be dramatically improved by increasing humus content and stimulating soil biological activity.

FIGURE 2. *Comparison of good crumb-like soil structure (left), with a poor, clod-like structure (right).*
(Drawing by Stewart Hoyt.)

A good crumb structure implies that soil is well aerated, since there will be plenty of pore spaces between the granules. Structure is also essential to the ability of soil to conduct soil moisture upward toward plant roots. This feature is referred to as capillary action, and it works in much the same way that oil is taken up into the wick of a lamp. If soil structure is good, the surface may dry out, but moisture will still reach the root zone from deeper soil levels. Adequate soil moisture is crucial not only to replenish what is lost through transpiration from plant leaves, but also because plant roots take up most of their nutrients when they are dissolved in the thin film of water that coats soil particles.

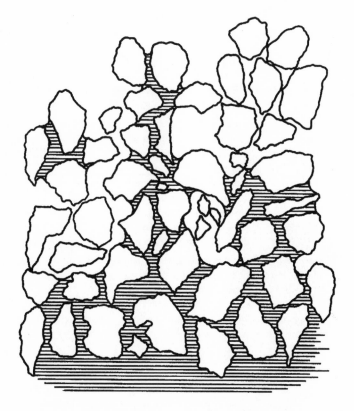

FIGURE 3. *Moisture moving upward in soil by capillary action.* (Drawing by Timothy Rice.)

Table 4

PHYSICAL PROPERTIES OF SOIL

Property and definition	Significance in soil	Influence of organic matter
Bulk Density: The weight of unit volume of dry soil, including pore spaces. Expressed as grams per cubic centimeter (gm/cm^3).	Indicates how dense the soil is and, therefore, how easily air, water, and plant roots can penetrate. (Optimum range: 1.0–1.8 gm/cm^3 for compact subsoil).	Increased organic matter leads to decreased bulk density, because organic matter is less dense than soil minerals and gas is released during decomposition.
Pore Space: The portion occupied by air and water per unit volume of soil. Expressed as a percentage of volume.	Indicates specific aeration and drainage qualities. (Optimum range: 35%–60% for topsoil; 25%–30% for compact subsoil.)	Increased organic matter leads to increased pore space. Soil organisms also increase pore space by burrowing and eating.
Structure and Aggregation: Refers to the arrangement of soil particles, their shape, size, and stability.	The structure that encourages the most plant growth is granular: rounded aggregates that stick together, but shake apart easily. Especially porous granules are called "crumbs."	Biological activity is virtually essential for proper granulation. Humus provides a perfect crumb structure that resists compaction.
Oxygen Diffusion Rate: The rate at which oxygen can be replenished as it is used by respiring organisms. Expressed as grams per cubic centimeter per minute ($gm/cm^3/min$).	Indicates the aeration status of the soil. In addition to pore space for air to enter, there must also be continual diffusion of fresh air into the soil to replace carbon dioxide with oxygen. (Minimum level for root growth is 20×10^{-8} $gm/cm^3/min$.)	Increased organic matter leads to an increased oxygen diffusion rate. Decomposing organic matter (especially plant roots) and mobile soil organisms create air passages in soil.
Field Capacity: The amount of water held in pore spaces after a fully saturated field has been allowed to drain for 24 hours. Expressed as a percentage of volume.	Indicates the drainage qualities of the soil. A low field capacity means that water runs out too quickly; with a high field capacity, water remains too long in pore spaces. (Well granulated silt loam has a field capacity of about 15%.)	By improving the soil structure, organic matter modulates the field capacity of soils that would otherwise be too wet or too dry.

CHEMICAL FACTORS: NUTRIENT CYCLES AND BALANCES

The conventional approach to soil management has been labeled "chemical," in contrast to the "organic" method, which rejects the use of synthetic, petrochemical fertilizers and pesticides. The chemical approach holds that plant roots require certain chemical nutrients, but how these nutrients get to the roots and where they come from matters little. The nutrient elements must be present in a soluble, inorganic form in order for plants to use them.

The ecological viewpoint holds that the effect of fertilizers on soil organisms and the environment is of equal importance to their value as plant food. "Feed the soil, not the plant," organic growers maintain, and soil organisms will provide a balanced diet to crops. Highly soluble chemicals, though readily taken up by plants, can inhibit or kill soil microbes, and can be washed away to pollute groundwater. Moreover, plants are also able to absorb and benefit from complex biochemicals such as vitamins and antibiotics, which are not present in artificially synthesized fertilizers.

Public concern over groundwater contamination by nitrate fertilizers, as well as other agrichemicals, has stimulated greater interest in soil management practices that do not rely on highly soluble materials.

Soil Chemistry Simplified

Regardless of which approach you adhere to—chemical or organic—the fundamentals of soil chemistry remain the same. Most chemical interactions, in the soil or anywhere else, take place between particles that carry either a positive or a negative charge when dissolved in water. Positively charged particles are called *cations* (pronounced "CAT-ions"), while *anions* ("AN-ions") carry a negative charge. These particles may be a single element, such as calcium (Ca^{2+}), or a compound, such as nitrate (NO_3^-). The behavior of nutrients in the soil ecosystem is determined by whether they exist as cations or anions.

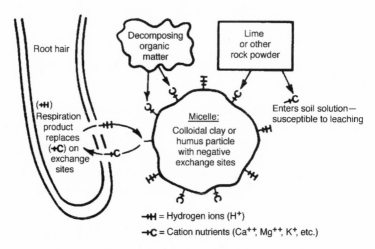

FIGURE 4. *Cation Exchange Capacity (CEC). The higher the CEC, the more nutrients can be kept available to plants, yet safe from leaching. Cations held on the exchange sites are said to be absorbed.*

The Basics of Cations

Cation nutrients tend to be metallic mineral elements, important for both plant and microbial nutrition as components of enzymes. They are generally quite water soluble, and enter the soil either through the recycling of organic matter or by addition of mineral nutrient sources such as limestone. Cations are called base elements because they form bases in solution. In humid climates, where there is over thirty inches of precipitation a year, cations tend to become leached out of the topsoil—more slowly if they are stored by soil colloids such as clay and humus. Soils in arid climates, conversely, are usually rich in minerals and so extremely productive when irrigated.

The major cation nutrients include calcium, magnesium, and potassium; their functions are summarized in the chart that follows. Other cation nutrients, needed in minute quantities, are described in the discussion of micronutrients (see page 23).

Table 5

MAJOR CATION NUTRIENTS

Nutrient	Natural sources	Forms in soil	Function in plants	Deficiency symptoms
Calcium (Ca^{2+})	Dolomite, calcite, apatite, calcium feldspars, gypsum.	Most is present as Ca^{2+} ion on cation exchange sites, or in soil solution. At high pH, calcium forms insoluble precipitates with phosphorus and some micronutrients.	Essential for nitrogen uptake and protein synthesis. Also has a role in enzyme activation and cell reproduction	Stunted root growth, undeveloped terminal buds, and leaf curl. Pit rot in carrots, blossom-end rot in tomatoes.
Magnesium (Mg^{2+})	Mica, hornblende, dolomite, serpentine, certain clays.	Present as Mg^{2+} ion on cation exchange sites, or in soil solution.	Essential part of chlorophyll molecule. Necessary for phosphorus metabolism and enzyme activation. Often concentrated in seeds.	Yellowing of lower leaves, with venation in green; reduced yields.
Potassium (K^+)	Feldspars, mica, granites, certain clays.	Available as K^+ on cation exchange sites or in soil solution. (Less than 1% of total soil K^+ is in available form.)	Essential for carbohydrate metabolism and cell division. Regulates absorption of calcium, sodium, and nitrogen.	Weakened stems, scorched leaf edges, necrotic spots, stunted growth, susceptible to disease.

CATION EXCHANGE CAPACITY

Cation Exchange Capacity, or CEC, is an important measurement of the amount of cation nutrients a given soil is able to store on its clay and humus colloid particles. Colloids, as described on page 25, have a large number of negatively charged sites all over their surface. Positively charged cations are held on these sites, largely protected from leaching away in water, but still available to plant roots. As plants give off hydrogen ions, a waste product that is also positively charged, it is exchanged for needed nutrients like calcium, magnesium, and potassium. Nutrients held in colloidal exchange sites may not show up in soil tests because they are not dissolved in water, but they are still available to plants through direct contact between roots and soil colloids. This process is referred to as adsorption.

Soils with a high clay and humus content will have the highest CEC, which is measured by how many thousandths of a gram of hydrogen—called milliequivalents—can be held by 100 grams of dry soil. Different kinds of clays have CECs ranging from 10 to as much as 100, while the CEC of pure humus can approach 200. Very sandy soils will have a CEC of 5 or less.

Think of your soil's CEC as a kind of nutrient savings account. As nutrients are "withdrawn," whether by removing crops or through the prolonged action of water, it is important to replace them in order to maintain your reserves. These reserves must be well stocked before plants are able to draw on them, so a soil with a high CEC but depleted nutrients will require greater applications of mineral nutrients to restore its fertility than will a similarly depleted but low CEC soil. A high CEC soil with an acid pH will require a larger amount of calcium, in the form of limestone, to correct it than will a low CEC soil with the same pH. Knowing your soil's CEC will help you better understand and interpret your soil test recommendations, as discussed in chapter 3.

COLLOIDS

One of the most important characteristics of humus is its colloidal nature. *Colloids* are substances composed of many tiny particles suspended in a gel-like mass, giving them a lot of surface area in proportion to their weight. Protein, which makes up all living cells, is a colloid. Other examples of colloids are milk, mayonnaise, rubber, and gelatin. Clay is also a colloid, and the clay component of the soil behaves similarly to humus. Physically, colloids tend to be sticky and absorbent.

Colloids are important chemically because they are covered with negatively charged particles. This makes them able to hold onto positively charged chemical particles, many of which are important soil nutrients. All soil chemical interactions are affected by the soil's clay-humus colloidal content.

Cations, pH and Fertility

When cation or base nutrients are deficient in soil, it becomes acid. pH (which stands for "potential hydrogen") is a measure of the acidity or alkalinity of soil, determined by the concentration of hydrogen ions in a water or salt solution. Acidity is indicated by a pH below 7.0, which is neutral; pH values over 7.0 indicate alkalinity.

As hydrogen ions replace the cation nutrients held in soil colloidal reserves, soil pH decreases. The solubility, and thus availability to plants, of most nutrients is highest at a slightly acid pH—around 6.3 to 6.8 is optimum. This is also the most favorable range for the functioning of most soil bacteria, though fungi can tolerate a wider pH range. At low pH—below 5.5—most major nutrients and some micronutrients assume insoluble forms. Phosphorus becomes chemically immobilized at both low and high pH, requiring a range between 6.0 and 7.0 for maximum availability.

Many cation micronutrients, including iron, manganese, zinc, copper, and cobalt, become more soluble at low pH but are unavailable under alkaline conditions. In some cases, acid conditions can induce toxicity of these elements. This is also true of certain heavy metals, most notably aluminum, which is naturally present in most soils, and lead, which can sometimes be a contaminant. Neutralizing the pH also neutralizes the heavy metal hazard.

When correcting soil acidity, the object is not so much to neutralize pH as it is to replenish the appropriate cation nutrients—usually calcium and sometimes magnesium in the form of limestone. Applying other alkaline materials, such as sodium bicarbonate, may neutralize the pH, but won't improve soil fertility.

"Acid soil syndrome" is a common problem in areas of high precipitation, where soluble soil bases tend to leach out into the subsoil. Some of the problems associated with acid soil include:

- Interference with the availability of nutrients to plants.
- Increased solubility of iron, manganese, and especially aluminum to undesirable levels.
- Reduced bacterial activity, especially of nitrogen-fixing rhizobia, and slower release of nutrients contained in organic matter.
- Lower total CEC, which further increases nutrients' leachability.

Alkaline soils can be even more difficult to correct. The addition of acid-forming minerals like sulfur is more expensive and temporary than the addition of limestone to acid soils. In many places where soil is naturally alkaline, improper irrigation practices may cause salts to build up in the surface layer, a condition known as **salinization**. This happens when nutrient-rich water rises to the surface through capillary action and then evaporates, leaving its minerals behind. Some soils in arid areas are naturally saline. It is difficult and costly to reverse these effects, and it is generally done by leaching the area with large amounts of fresh water—a resource usually in short supply in affected regions.

Among the problems associated with alkaline soils are:

- Unavailability of many nutrients, especially most micronutrients.
- Saline seep, causing soil crusting.
- Toxic levels of sodium, selenium, and other minerals.
- Chemical destruction of organic matter.

Soil Anions and Their Cycles

Anion nutrients differ from cations in that they are not stored chemically by soil colloids, and form acids in solution. Reserves of anion nutrients are held in the organic portion of the soil, and are released to plants through the decay of organic matter or through the air and water. Depending on the status of soil organisms and the decay cycle, soil anions continually change in form and quantity. As the major building blocks of proteins and carbohydrates, anions are required in larger quantities than are cation nutrients. It is helpful to think of anions as large, soft, and changeable in form, while cations are small, hard, and durable.

When added to the soil as soluble fertilizers, anion nutrients may be lost because they volatilize into the atmosphere, leach away, or revert to more stable, insoluble forms. These soluble fertilizers may be acid-forming, or otherwise harmful to soil organisms. When substituted for nutrient sources rich in organic matter, they can be likened to an addiction: Higher doses will be required to replace the nutrients that were previously supplied naturally by the soil's ecosystem.

- **Nitrogen** tends naturally toward the gaseous state as its most stable and plentiful form. The nitrate form, in which it is present in the soil solution, is extremely transitory and will fluctuate significantly from day to day and even at different times of day. Although plants cannot use atmospheric nitrogen directly, certain soil microbes, most notably the rhizobia

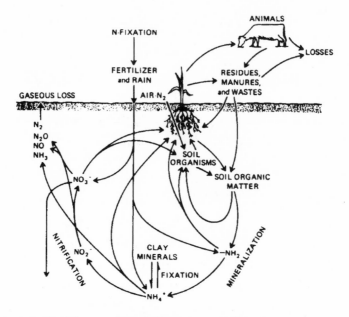

FIGURE 5. *The Nitrogen Cycle. Plants cannot utilize nitrogen in its gaseous form. In order to pass from atmosphere to plant (and then to animals and people), nitrogen must first be fixed by soil microorganisms. To make synthetic fertilizers, atmosheric nitrogen is artifically fixed through use of huge quantities of natural gas. (33,000 to 40,000 cubic feet of natural gas is required to produce one ton of ammonia.)*

Reprinted with permission of MacMillan Publishing Company from *The Nature and Properties of Soils*, 8th Ed., by Nyle C. Brady. Copyright 1974 by MacMillan Publishing Company.

bacteria that live on the roots of legumes, are able to capture it from the air and transform it into a biologically useful form. Free-living soil bacteria such as azotobacter and clostridia are even more important for nitrogen fixation. Still other bacteria transform the nitrogen from ammonium to nitrite and then to nitrate form; each step in the natural nitrogen cycle is essential for plant nutrition.

• **Carbon,** the major constituent of plant (and animal) tissue, is more truly the "food" consumed by plants than any mineral. Although abundant in the organic fraction of the soil, carbon

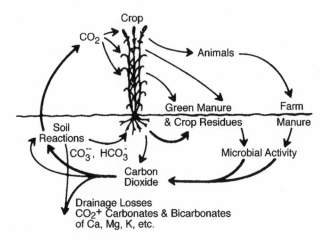

FIGURE 6. *The Carbon Cycle. Gaseous carbon dioxide is transformed by plants into living tissue. Carbohydrates, proteins, and fats are decomposed by soil organisms, thereby replenishing the supply of atmospheric carbon dioxide.*

Reprinted with permission of MacMillan Publishing Company from *The Nature and Properties of Soils*, 8th Ed., by Nyle C. Brady. Copyright 1974 by MacMillan Publishing Company.

is taken in by plants almost entirely from the atmosphere, as carbon dioxide. The carbon dioxide concentration close to the ground can be substantially enriched by the presence of actively decaying organic matter, which directly stimulates plant growth. Lack of carbon dioxide can be a problem in greenhouses, where air circulation must be artificially maintained. An indoor compost pile can add carbon dioxide—and extra heat—to the greenhouse environment.

- **Phosphorus** undergoes some of the most complex chemical interactions of all the elements of soil fertility. It is easily immobilized in the soil through its tendency to form insoluble compounds with calcium and other minerals. At a pH near neutral, even highly soluble phosphorus fertilizers will soon revert to forms indistinguishable from the "natural" rock powders from which they were manufactured. Once added to the soil, immobilized phosphorus stays there a long time;

Table 6

MAJOR ANION NUTRIENTS

Nutrient	Natural sources	Forms in soil	Function in plants	Deficiency symptoms
Carbon (C)	Organic matter, respiration of soil organisms.	Organic compounds, carbon dioxide gas in air spaces, and weak carbonic acids.	Basic constituent of all living cells.	If atmospheric carbon dioxide is limited, plant growth is slowed.
Nitrogen (N)	Organic matter, atmospheric nitrogen fixed by microbes, small amounts dissolved in rain water.	Organic compounds, nitrites, nitrates, and ammonium (soluble forms).	Basic constituent of protein and genetic material.	Thin stems; yellowing (chlorosis) of leaves, beginning with lower leaves; slowed growth.
Phosphorus (P)	Organic matter, mineral powders, some parent materials.	Organic compounds; soluble phosphates; insoluble compounds of iron, aluminum, manganese, magnesium, and calcium.	Essential for genetic material, membrane formation, and energy transfer.	Purpling of leaves, beginning on undersides; stunted roots; slowed growth.
Sulfur (S)	Organic matter, atmospheric sulfur fixed by microbes, pollutants in rain water.	Organic compounds; soluble sulfates, sulfites, and sulfides.	Important constituent of proteins and certain vitamins.	Deficiency is hard to detect, but resembles nitrogen deficiency, with yellowing of whole plant.

many soils, especially in the Midwest, have phosphorus reserves created by government encouragement of excessive fertilizer applications.

Phosphorus is most readily available to plants when released gradually through the decomposition of organic matter. Its relative immobility means that distribution of phosphorus throughout the soil is only accomplished through the movement of earthworms and other soil organisms. Otherwise, insoluble soil phosphorus reserves can become available to plants through the activities of soil microbes.

• **Sulfur,** an essential component of protein and fats, acts much like nitrogen in the soil ecosystem and is particularly important for nitrogen-fixing microorganisms. A special group of microbes transforms organic sulfur into the sulfate form utilized by plants. Sulfur deficiency is rarely a problem, especially where adequate soil organic matter levels are maintained. Air pollution also has had unintended beneficial effects on the sulfur content of soils downwind. Deficiencies have risen with increased use of highly concentrated phosphate and nitrate fertilizers, which lack the sulfur impurities found in the lower grades. Sulfur is often needed as a nutrient and an acidifier for alkaline soils.

Micronutrients

Micronutrients are elements that are important in very small amounts for the proper functioning of biological systems. Sometimes called "trace elements," over a dozen of them have been identified as essential in minute quantities for plant, animal, or microbial enzyme functions. Most of the important micronutrients, such as iron, zinc, copper, and manganese, are cations; boron and molybdenum are the most important anion micronutrients.

Micronutrients occur, in cells as well as in soil, as part of large, complex organic molecules in chelated form. The word *chelate* (pronounced "KEE-late") comes from the Greek word for "claw," which indicates how a single nutrient ion is held in the center of the larger molecule. The finely balanced interactions between micronutrients are complex and not fully understood. We do know that balance is crucial; any micronutrient, when present in excessive amounts, will become a poison, and certain poisonous elements, such as chlorine, are also essential micronutrients.

For this reason natural, organic sources of micronutrients are the best means of supplying them to the soil: they are present in balanced quantities and not liable to be overapplied through error or ignorance. When used in naturally chelated form, excess micronutrients will be locked up and prevented from disrupting soil balances. Soil humus reserves also serve to chelate excess metals—nutrients as well as toxins. Unless a specific micronutrient deficiency has been diagnosed by a soil test, the best way to provide adequate supplies is by building organic matter and applying balanced sources of minerals such as rock powders and seaweed. See chapter 4 for more information on micronutrient fertilizers.

FIGURE 7. *Chelation illustrated by the chlorophyll molecule.*

Table 7

SOME IMPORTANT MICRONUTRIENTS

Nutrient	Desired amount in soil (ppm)*	Function in plants	Deficiency symptoms
Iron (Fe)	25,000	Chlorophyll synthesis, oxidation, constituent of various enzymes and proteins.	Chlorosis (yellowing), larger veins remain green; short and slender stems.
Manganese (Mn)	2,500	Synthesis of chlorophyll and several vitamins, carbohydrate and nitrogen metabolism.	Yellow mottling of leaves, pale overall coloring, poor maturation and keeping quality.
Zinc (Zn)	100	Formation of growth hormones, protein synthesis, seed and grain production and maturation.	Late summer mottling of leaves. Early defoliation of fruit trees.
Copper (Cu)	50	Catalyst for enzyme and chlorophyll synthesis, respiration, carbohydrate and protein metabolism.	Yellowing and elongation of leaves. Onions are soft, with pale yellow scales.
Boron (B)	50	Protein synthesis, starch and sugar transport, root development, fruit and seed formation, water uptake and transport.	Growing tips die back. Heart rot of root crops, corky core of apples, poor legume nitrogen fixation.
Molybdenum (Mo)	2	Essential for symbiotic nitrogen fixation and protein synthesis.	Pale, distorted, narrow leaves, leaf roll, poor nitrogen fixation.

*Approximate values indicate relative proportions.

A Balancing Act

Balance is the crucial concept for understanding the relationship between chemical nutrients and soil fertility. Fertility requires not only sufficient quantities of nutrients, but their presence in balanced form. In many cases, too much of one nutrient will lock up or interfere with the absorption of another. Phosphorus is the classic example; it will become immobilized at low pH by high concentrations of zinc and iron, and at high pH by too much calcium. Potassium and magnesium will each interfere with the availability of the other, when present in excess. In the case of carbon and nitrogen, too much

Table 8

NUTRIENT INTERACTIONS

Nutrient	Deficiency may be induced by excess of	Excess may induce deficiency of
CATIONS		
Calcium	Aluminum	Magnesium, potassium, iron, manganese, zinc, phosphorus, boron
Magnesium	Calcium, potassium, ammonium	Potassium, zinc, boron, manganese
Potassium	Magnesium, calcium, ammonium	Magnesium, boron
Iron	Phosphorus (high pH), manganese (low pH), calcium, copper, aluminum, zinc	Zinc, manganese
Manganese	Iron, copper, zinc, calcium, magnesium	Iron
Zinc	Phosphorus, nitrogen, magnesium, iron, copper, calcium, aluminum	Iron, copper, manganese
Copper	Phosphorus, zinc, nitrogen	Iron, zinc, manganese
ANIONS		
Carbon	Sulfur, nitrogen, phosphorus	Sulfur, nitrogen, phosphorus
Nitrogen	Carbon, phosphorus	Phosphorus
Phosphorus	Calcium, nitrogen, iron, aluminum, manganese	Zinc, copper, nitrogen
Sulfur	Carbon, nitrogen	
Boron	Calcium, potassium	
Molybdenum	Sulfur, copper	Iron, copper

carbon will stimulate soil microbes to grow and take up all the available soil nitrogen, resulting in a temporary deficiency until the microbes die and release their nutrients to the soil system.

Cation balances have received a lot of scientific attention. **Base saturation** refers to the percentage of a soil's CEC (see box, page 24) occupied by bases—cations other than hydrogen or aluminum.

Some efforts have been made to find the "ideal" cation balance or base saturation ratio. One very influential scientist was Dr. William Albrecht, who conducted research at the University of Missouri in the 1940s. Albrecht's key contribution was to point out the importance of calcium as a major ingredient of fertility, contending that it was the calcium in limestone, not its acid-neutralizing ability, that made it an important fertilizer. He also developed a formula for an optimum base saturation ratio, emphasizing calcium, which has been used by many soil labs to evaluate mineral balances. While it is a useful guideline, Albrecht's ratio is not universally accurate, and should not be relied on exclusively to determine fertilizer needs.

The ideal proportion of anion nutrients is the balance that is normally found in humus: 100 parts carbon to 10 parts nitrogen to 1 part phosphorus to 1 part sulfur. The importance of the carbon to nitrogen ratio was described earlier; however, the ratio of nitrogen to phosphorus is also important to proper plant nutrition, since inadequate nitrogen slows the growth of roots and therefore their ability to reach phosphorus supplies.

Micronutrient problems are as often a result of imbalances as of absolute deficiencies. New information is continually being discovered about previously unknown interactions between major and minor nutrients in the soil ecosystem. This is why the "cookbook" approach to soil chemistry can get you into trouble; the best nutrient sources are those that are naturally balanced. The chart on page 34 will give you some indication of the complexity of known nutrient interactions.

BIOLOGICAL FACTORS: The Living Soil Community

The cycles that permit nutrients to flow from soil to plant are all interdependent, and proceed only with the help of the living organisms that constitute the soil community. Soil microorganisms are the essential link between mineral reserves and plant growth. Animals and people are also part of this community. Unless their wastes are returned to the soil, for the benefit of the organisms that live there, the whole life-supporting process will be undermined.

Soil organisms—from bacteria and fungi to protozoans and nematodes, on up to mites, springtails, and earthworms—perform a vast array of fertility maintenance tasks. Ecological soil management aims at assisting these creatures in their work, rather than substituting a simplified chemical system to provide nutrients to plants. For, once disrupted by the excessive use of soluble fertilizers, the restoration of a healthy soil ecosystem can be a long and costly process.

Soil Inhabitants

Microscopic plants and animals form the basis for the soil food web. Most contribute directly to humus formation and the release of nutrients from organic matter. Stable humus, in fact, consists largely of microbial remains. In cool, humid climates, fungi and molds are more significant than bacteria for humus development. Beyond their importance for soil health, these microbial decomposers are essential to all life on Earth, since they are responsible for virtually all organic waste recycling.

Other creatures, both microscopic and visible, make important contributions to soil health, most notably the earthworm. Plant roots themselves are major participants in the soil ecosystem, and significantly affect the environment that sustains them. Once you become aware of the astonishing number and variety of life forms that are constantly growing, reproducing, and dying in every crumb of soil—billions in each gram of healthy topsoil—it is impossible to pick up a handful of earth without feeling a sense of awe. Each organism has a role to play in the soil ecosystem:

- **Producers** create carbohydrates and proteins from simple nutrient elements, almost always by capturing energy from sunlight through photosynthesis. Green plants, including blue-green algae, are the producers of the soil. A few specialized bacteria, known as **autotrophs,** are also able to synthesize their own food from carbon dioxide and mineral elements in the soil.

- **Consumers** are just about everyone else, who all depend on the food created by green plants for their nourishment. Primary consumers eat plants directly, while secondary and tertiary consumers feed on other consumers. All animal life, from simple protozoans to humans, as well as nonphotosynthesizing plants, such as yeasts and certain other fungi, fall into this category.

- **Decomposers** perform the critical function of bringing the basic chemical nutrients full circle, from consumers back to producers. They are all bacteria or fungi, and are found almost exclusively in the soil; about 60 to 80 percent of the total soil metabolism is accounted for by microbial decomposers. Without them, life would grind to a halt as we suffocated in our own wastes.

What They Need

If the surest route to improving soil fertility is to provide the most hospitable conditions for soil life, understanding the basic needs of soil organisms is the first step. Successful composting requires the same knowledge: Provide soil beasties with adequate food, air, and water, and—depending on other environmental factors, such as temperature—they will flourish.

Table 9

SOIL ORGANISMS

Organism	Approximate soil population	Special requirements	Source of nutrition	Role in ecosystem
MICROFLORA				
Fungi: yeast, molds, mycorrhizae.	10^5–10^6 per gram	Will tolerate wide pH and temperature ranges.	Organic matter or nutrients from plant roots.	Humus formation, and aggregate stabilization. Create antibiotics, cause plant diseases, make phosphorus available.
Actinomycetes.	10^7–10^8 per gram	Need aeration, moisture, and pH 6.0–7.5.	Organic matter.	Humus formation.
Bacteria Autotrophs: *Azotobacter, Rhizobia, Nitrobacter.* **Heterotrophs:** decay organisms.	10^8–10^9 per gram	Most need air (aerobes), and exchangeable calcium. Temperature of 70°–100°F, pH 6–8.	Autotrophs consume simple nutrients from soil and air. Heterotrophs break down organic matter.	Autotrophs are nitrogen-fixers, sulfur oxidizers, nitrifiers. Some cause disease. Heterotrophs are decomposers.
Algae: green, blue-green.	10^4–10^5 per gram		Photosynthesis.	Add organic matter to soil. Some fix nitrogen.
MICROFAUNA				
Nematodes.	10–100 per gram		Organic matter, other microbes, plant roots.	Secondary consumers. Some are pests and parasites.
Protozoa, rotifers.	10^4–10^5 per gram			
INSECTS & MOLLUSCS				
Mites, springtails, spiders, sowbugs, ants, beetles, centipedes, millipedes, slugs, snails.	10^3–10^5 per m^2		Microflora, microfauna, other insects, plant roots and residues, nematodes, molluscs, detritus (waste matter), organic matter, weak plants.	Aerate and mix soil. Leave remains for decomposers. Cull weak or diseased plants.

Table 9 (continued)

SOIL ORGANISMS

Organism	Approximate soil population	Special requirements	Source of nutrition	Role in ecosystem
		EARTHWORMS		
Earthworms.	30–300 per m²	Raw organic matter.	Aerate and mix soil.	Leave nutrient-rich casts.
		MAMMALS		
Moles, mice, goundhogs.	Variable	Earthworms, insects, molluscs.		Mix and pulverize soil. Leave wastes.
		PLANT ROOTS		
Roots.	100–6,000 lbs. per acre.		Photosynthesis; nutrient ions and molecules.	Remove water and nutrients; leave residues and exudates.

Both soil and compost creatures need the same food: raw organic matter with a balanced ratio of carbon to nitrogen—approximately 25 or 30 parts to 1. Carbon, in the form of carbohydrates, is really the main course for soil organisms: they will grow quickly given lots of it, and will scavenge every scrap of nitrogen from the soil system to go with it. That's why adding lots of high-carbon materials to your soil can cause nitrogen deficiencies in plants. In the long term, though, carbon is the ultimate fuel for all soil biological activity, and is therefore crucial to humus formation and plant productivity. A balanced supply of mineral nutrients is also essential for soil beasties, and micronutrients are key to the many bacterial enzymes involved in their biochemical transformations. Balanced nutrients also provide a favorable pH, though different organisms are more sensitive to acid or alkaline conditions.

Air is also crucial for soil health, although certain bacteria can live without it (see box, page 42). In fact, much effort in soil management is directed toward improving soil aeration: no amount of fertilizing can compensate for lack of air, since plant roots cannot take full advantage of available nutrients if they are suffocating.

Water is also strictly essential, but not to the extent that it drives out air. The ideal biological environment consists of a thin film of moisture clinging to each soil particle, with lots of air circulating between them. Rain and irrigation, of course, play a central role in adding needed soil moisture, but good structure is also required to conduct moisture upward from reserves in lower soil strata (see page 19).

Although temperature has critical effects on biological activity, every specific soil community has evolved to accommodate the natural climate variations in its environment. Your only role in adjusting the temperature might be to moderate severe winter cold or summer heat by mulching, or to heat up small areas with season extension devices.

Soil Superstars

Despite the many volumes that have been written about soil biology, knowledge of the kinds of organisms that live in soil and how they interact is extremely limited. Although some scientists have tried to work out biological assays to identify a soil's characteristics and needs by examining its living population, such tests are still extremely complex to carry out and difficult to interpret accurately.

The table on pages 38–39 summarizes the major types of soil life forms. A few portraits of the more familiar and celebrated soil inhabitants, in order of size, follows:

Bacteria: Bacteria are the most numerous and varied of soil organisms, ranging from a few hundred million to three billion in every gram of soil. Under the right conditions they can double their population every hour. The top six to eight inches of soil may contain anywhere from a couple of hundred pounds to two tons of live bacteria per acre.

Bacteria vary in their requirement for air, but most beneficial ones need it (see box, page 42). If enough moisture and food are present, bacteria do best at temperatures of 70° to 100°F (21° to 38°C), and at a pH close to neutral. Adequate calcium is crucial, as is a balance of micronutrients, which are essential to the enzymes em-

The three most important plant microorganisms of the soil. Fungal mycelium (left), various types of bacteria cells (center), and actinomycetes threads (right). The bacteria and antinomycetes are much more highly magnified than the fungus.

Parasitic nematodes (left), a ciliated protozoan (center), and a common rotifer (right).

Some soil organisms especially important in the nitrogen cycle. Azotobacter (left), nitrate bacteria (center), and nodule organisms of alfalfa (right).

FIGURE 8. *Important Soil Organisms.*
(Drawing by Timothy Rice)

ployed by bacteria to perform their crucial biochemical tasks. Unfavorable conditions rarely kill bacteria off completely; they will either stop growing and form spores to wait for better times, or adapt to the changed conditions as genetic mutations quickly spread to new generations. This adaptability can work against you when the organism in question causes a plant disease, though. If any soil nutrient is in limited supply, bacteria will be the first to consume it; plants then must wait to partake until the microbes die and decompose.

BACTERIA AND BREATHING

The soil micro-universe is divided into two general types of bacteria: those that need air and those that don't. The availability of air thus determines which kinds of bacteria will flourish, and how vigorously they will grow.

- Aerobes require air in order to live. The bacteria that mediate the soil nitrogen and sulfur cycles, as well as many important decomposers, are aerobes. All other soil organisms are also aerobic, including plant roots. Some bacteria can survive in either aerobic or anaerobic conditions, but will only grow and thrive if they have air.

- Anaerobes can live happily without air, and in fact may be killed if exposed to it. The bacteria responsible for diseases like botulism and tetanus are famous examples. There are many anaerobic decomposers, which often generate some foul-smelling waste products, such as hydrogen sulfide, and the common term for the process of anaerobic decomposition is **putrefaction.** Anaerobic bacteria can also generate useful by-products such as methane gas, which is sometimes used as an energy source.

Bacteria have a virtual monopoly on three basic soil processes that are vital to higher plants: nitrification, sulfur oxidation, and nitrogen fixation. Nitrifying bacteria transform nitrogen in the form of ammonium, a product of protein decomposition, into nitrate, the form most available to plants. The sulfur oxidation process is analogous to nitrification. Nitrogen-fixing bacteria are able to transform elemental nitrogen from the atmosphere into protein, and eventually make it available to other organisms—a process imitated by humans at a high energy cost. They may live in symbiosis with plant roots, such as the members of the Rhizobium family, or they may be free-living soil dwellers, such as *Azotobacter*.

Fungi: Yeasts, molds, and mushrooms are all fungi, and only yeasts have little presence in the soil. Although they are plants, they do not contain chlorophyll and so must depend on other plants for their nourishment. Molds may be as numerous as bacteria in soil, and will outnumber them under conditions of poor aeration, low temperature, and acidity, which they tolerate more easily. Although many plant diseases are caused by soil-dwelling molds such as *Fusarium* and *Aspergillus*, those in the *Penicillium* family are well known as disease fighters. Molds are especially important for humus formation, predominating in humus-rich, acid forest soils.

FIGURE 9. *Mycorrhizae infecting a plant root and extracting nutrients from rock particles.*
(Drawing by Timothy Rice.)

One extremely significant group of fungi are called mycorrhizae, a term meaning "fungus root." These mushrooms enter into symbiotic relationships with plant roots of many kinds, and are thought to be essential for the health of trees such as pine and birch. The fungi are able to convert otherwise insoluble nutrients, most notably phosphorus, into biological forms, and in turn receive carbohydrates from their host plants. Many crop plants are known to enter into **mycorrhizal associations,** but they are most significant for plants growing on poor soils, where the fungal ability to extract nutrients from rock particles is most critical to the host plant's nutrition.

Actinomycetes: These microbes are like a cross between bacteria and fungi, and are the most numerous soil organisms after bacteria. The characteristic aroma of freshly plowed earth is attributed to actinomycetes, which play a critical role in organic matter decomposition and humus formation. They need plenty of air and a pH between 6.0 and 7.5, but are more tolerant than either bacteria or fungi of dry conditions. Their intolerance of low pH can be used to advantage in preventing potato scab, a disease caused by an actinomycete. Manure is especially rich in actinomycetes, which is why many people consider manure to be essential for making high-quality compost.

Algae: Algae are single-celled plants, usually containing chlorophyll, and are slightly less numerous in the soil than are fungi. Blue-green algae are common in many kinds of soils, but are particularly important in paddy rice culture because of their tolerance for high moisture levels and their ability to fix atmospheric nitrogen. All algae growth is greatly stimulated by farm manure.

Microfauna: Microscopic soil animals including nematodes, protozoans, and rotifers. Nematodes, commonly called threadworms or eelworms, are extremely widespread and numerous in most soils.

PLANT-MICROBE SYMBIOSIS

The mutually beneficial relationships between plant roots and soil microbes are complex and widely varied. Some of these arrangements are well understood, but many remain mysterious. As we learn more about the workings of these microorganisms, they will undoubtedly be used more widely to improve crop production.

A few bacteria are able to convert nitrogen gas from the air into a form usable by the roots of the plant with which they associate. *Rhizobium* bacteria, for example, form visible nodules on the roots of legumes, whose growth is greatly enhanced by the nitrogen fixed there. When the legumes are returned to the soil, as with green manure crops, the nitrogen fixed by the rhizobia becomes available to the subsequent crop (see table 17). When a legume is grown in association with another crop, for example grasses or grains, the nitrogen fixed by the rhizobia is available to the associated crop while the two are growing together. Because not all soils contain these desirable nitrogen-fixing bacteria, when farmers plant legumes they often inoculate either their soil or seed with preparations containing rhizobia.

Other soil organisms, such as the actinomycete *Frankia,* the bacteria *Azotobacter,* and some blue-green algae, are likewise capable of fixing nitrogen, with and without host species.

It has been estimated that more than 80 percent of plants have symbiotic associations with fungal mycorrhizae, whose pervasive filaments extend the reach of plant roots in the soil, often improving the roots' ability to absorb nutrients. Some of these mycorrhizae are relatively nonspecific, able to penetrate the roots of many different species of plants in various ecosystems. Others are quite specific, surrounding the roots of only one plant species in one type of soil.

Although they are often thought of as troublesome plant pests, the most common kinds help break down organic matter or prey on bacteria, algae, or other soil animals. Some parasitic nematodes are used as biological control agents for soil-dwelling pests such as cabbage root maggots. Protozoans are one-celled animals that are larger than bacteria, often using them as a food supply. Rotifers are common in wet soils, feeding by spinning around and sweeping food particles into their "mouths."

Earthworms and Other Macrofauna: Of the numerous animals who make their homes in the soil, from miniscule spiders to prairie dogs, the earthworm is the most closely identified with soil health (see box, "The Noble Worm"). Other small soil animals include mites and spiders, beetles, springtails, flies, termites, ants, centipedes, and slugs, as well as the larval forms of many butterflies and moths. Many of these creatures play an important role in breaking down organic materials into smaller pieces and simpler compounds; some are significant as plant pests. Mammals such as moles, voles, gophers, and other burrowers can sometimes be a nuisance when they decide your broccoli looks good to them; however, they too contribute to the soil ecosystem by keeping pest populations in check, mixing soil, and depositing their droppings.

Farm Animals: The importance of farm animals to soil fertility sometimes gets overlooked. Although modern "factory farming" concentrates too many animals on small areas, the ideal farming system should include some animals. Besides contributing valuable manure, farm animals are important for a number of ecological soil-building practices:

- Soil-building rotations require sod crops and legumes, which are often only economically feasible when used as animal feed.

- Animals are often the only means to harvest a crop (besides trees) on soils that are too wet, steeply sloping, or stony to cultivate.

- Pigs and chickens can improve the soil by acting as living rototillers, scratching and aerating a patch before crops are planted. They also eat weeds and ground-dwelling pests.

THE NOBLE WORM

A good earthworm population is universally considered a sign of healthy soil. Unparalleled as soil excavators, earthworms spend their lives ingesting, grinding, digesting, and excreting soil: as much as fifteen tons of soil per acre goes through earthworm bodies in a year. Earthworm castings are richer in nutrients and bacteria than the surrounding soil, and may add up to as much as eight tons of nutrients per acre in cultivated fields. Their contribution to drainage and aeration, soil aggregation, and transport of nutrients from the subsoil is significant as well. It is for good reason that Charles Darwin extolled earthworms as the "intestines of the soil."

Of about two hundred known earthworm species, *Lumbricus terrestris* is the most common: interestingly enough, it is not native to North America, but came with the Europeans and turned out to be better adapted to cultivated conditions than its native predecessor. Earthworms, unlike the types of worms used for composting, prefer cool temperatures—about 50°F (10°C) is optimum. They need good aeration and enough but not too much moisture. Although some species can tolerate fairly acid soils, most require adequate calcium supplies and thus more neutral pH. They are also sensitive to many toxic pest- and weed-control chemicals, as well as fertilizers with a high salt index.

Life in the Root Zone

Plant roots themselves play an important role in soil ecology. The largest numbers and kinds of organisms are found in the uppermost layers of the soil, closer to fresh sources of air, water, and food. True, some biological activity happens even at fairly deep levels, especially where earthworms and other animals burrow, and where deep-rooted plants grow. However, in the area immediately surrounding plant roots, known as the **rhizosphere,** there are concentrations of ten to as many as one hundred times more organisms than can be found elsewhere in the soil. A soil such as that found under permanent grass sod, totally permeated by fibrous masses of roots, will inevitably have a healthier, more robust microbial population than one with cleanly cultivated row crops.

Most of the important soil biological transformations take place in the rhizosphere, especially nitrogen fixation and mycorrhizal associations. The outer coating of the growing root tip, called the **mucigel,** is a fascinating substance, a product of both the root and the microcommunity around it. A gelatinous substance secreted by the root, the mucigel is a rich mass of microbes and chemical nutrients that connects the plant directly to the life of the soil.

Some ways in which plant roots interact with the rest of the soil community include:

- Roots can take up cation nutrients directly from exchange sites on soil particles in exchange for hydrogen, through a process known as **adsorption** (see page 24).

- Plant roots give off carbon dioxide in the process of respiration, just as animals do. Together with the release of hydrogen described above, this creates slightly more acid conditions in the rhizosphere, since carbon dioxide forms a weak acid when dissolved in water. This slight acidity helps to make otherwise insoluble phosphorus and micronutrients more available.

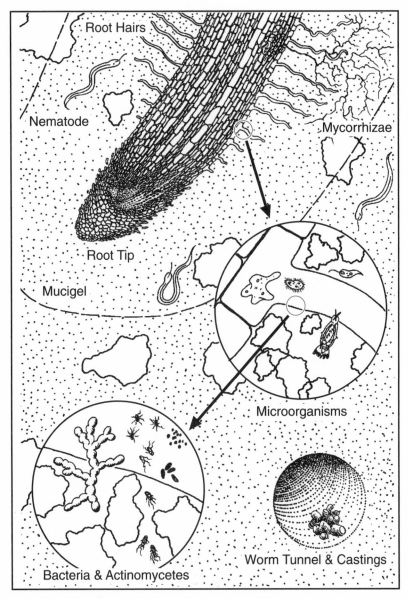

FIGURE 10. *The rhizosphere, a region approximately 3mm wide, and the zone of highest biological and chemical activity where soil, root, and microbes interact. Mucigel is a gelatinous substance surrounding the root that is both the mediator and the product of the root-soil-microbe community.* (Drawing by Timothy Rice.)

- Roots give off certain biochemical compounds called **exudates,** which sometimes act as **phytotoxins,** chemical inhibitors of competing plant species—a process called **allelopathy.** Winter rye, for example, gives off exudates that suppress couchgrass growth.

- The dead tissue continually sloughed off by growing roots is excellent food for microorganisms. The organic contribution of the root portion of a green manure crop often is more substantial than the part you see above the surface.

- Plant roots are able to take up many complex organic compounds such as hormones, vitamins, antibiotics, and humus fractions, as well as toxic substances like pesticides and herbicides. This is an important counter to the argument that the source of plant nutrients—whether chemical fertilizers or compost—is irrelevant to plant health.

Soil and Civilization

All land-dwelling animals, including humans, are members of the soil community. Human societies disregard this fact at their own peril: soil fertility has historically been squandered for the immediate enrichment of a few at the expense of future generations. Cultural values—ethics, aesthetics, and spiritual beliefs—have a profound influence on how soil is treated.

Not only the farm itself, but also the society of which it is a part must be viewed as components of the soil ecosystem, for all support and maintain one another and none can exist independently. Without a good-sized nonfarm community nearby, for example, marketing becomes a problem for the farmer; yet too large a nonfarm community exerts pressure to convert productive farmland to other uses. A whole book could be written about the effects of political and economic pressures on soil fertility—especially in the "Third World," where peasants are forced to produce export crops for foreign exchange instead of food for their families.

The 1992 United Nations Earth Summit acknowledged the importance of sustainable agriculture as a means of reversing worldwide environmental degradation. Implementing its recommendations will require widespread public consciousness-raising. Political and social activism are, more clearly than ever, essential components of soil stewardship.

OBSERVING AND
EVALUATING YOUR SOIL

Conventional agriculture has frequently confused means and ends, establishing "goals" such as a 150-bushel corn yield, then testing soil nutrient levels for comparison with levels "known" to be appropriate to the desired yield. Commonly, both the target corn yield and the associated target soil nutrient levels are considered in complete isolation from the broader ecological, economic, and family situation of which they are a part. Blatant conflict of interest is far from rare, as it is often the fertilizer company doing the sampling and making the recommendations as a "service" to the farmer.

In ecological agriculture, by way of comparison, the farm family's goal may well be some variation on the following:

A happy, healthy, and prosperous farm in a clean, vital, and diverse rural environment.

Soil testing, and other tests as well, become tools to evaluate how well the farm system is moving toward the different components of this goal.

RECORDKEEPING

To be a good farmer or gardener, you must be a keen observer of nature, and you must be able to use your observations to improve your management practices. Hence the truism, "The best fertilizer is the footprint of the farmer." You may try out a technique developed at a research station, borrow an idea from a neighbor, or simply follow a hunch. The skill lies in judging how well it works for you.

One of the most important tools of soil management is an accurate set of records. Your farm is unique: what works elsewhere may not work the same way here. To evaluate a new method, you try it under different conditions, keep track of the results, and then compare. This is the essence of the scientific method—what an experienced farmer might call common sense.

Your recordkeeping system should be a good match with the level of complexity of your farm system. You should be able to track the progress of livestock, crop production, processed products, farmstand sales, or orchard management separately. There are many computer-based recordkeeping and farm planning systems available to help you evaluate the financial results of your management decisions. The financial viability of any farm rests to a large extent on your ability to make changes based on information in your records.

Maps are one of the primary farm recordkeeping tools. Aerial photos, used to verify participation in federal conservation programs, are often available from the Soil Conservation Service, and can be useful in preparing an overall map of your farm. Your map should show the relative location and size of each field unit, building, waterway, road, and other significant features. Include as much detail as possible about slopes, rocky outcroppings, wet areas, and other characteristics critical to how the land is used. This map should be big enough to note what crop is being grown in each field: keep a master and photocopy it every season so you can look back at a glance to find each field's cropping history.

Some kind of journal is helpful for keeping track of information as it comes up, such as weather (especially rainfall), pest, weed, and disease problems, and crop growth and development, as well as your management activities: planting and transplanting, cultivating, pruning, spraying foliar nutrients, fertilizing, and harvesting. Refer to your map to indicate where something happened, whenever appropriate.

A diary format works well for much of this recordkeeping, and also allows you to reflect on the possible causes of problems and to make note of ideas for improvement as they come up. Some people use a large wall calendar to record activities, as well as to remind themselves of what needs doing when. A looseleaf notebook, with separate pages for each field or rotation unit, can help you find out quickly when a given area has had a green manure crop or compost application. You can also have a page describing the yearly soil observations you've made, along with copies of your soil test results.

One section of your notebook can be devoted to background information about your farm. Ask your local Soil Conservation Service office for the most recent soil survey for your county (not every county has complete surveys available). This will include extensive information about your soil type and its suitability for different uses. Drainage characteristics, geological information (such as effects of glaciation and type of bedrock), and slope are all described in detail.

The EQIP, or Environmental Quality Improvement Program, was recently established by USDA's Natural Resources Conservation Service (NRCS). Participation in this program entails comprehensive whole-farm planning that includes some valuable evaluation and monitoring of soil quality. Contact your local NRCS office for information.

Beyond just your land, it helps to know about your own bioregion—the area defined by common ecological factors. Elevation, temperature and precipitation patterns, waterways, and the types of vegetation and wildlife that predominate in your region are all important pieces of information. Where do the prevailing winds come from, and how strong are they? Is there a nearby lake that moderates temperatures? When it is put together, this information can help you make better educated guesses about the sources of problems or the probable success of a new farm crop.

If you are interested in organic certification, getting into a good recordkeeping habit is crucial. Extensive and detailed records are a key requirement of every bona fide organic certification program. You need to be able to go back at least three years in your soil management history, and show what fertility improvement and pest control measures you have used. Keep receipts for any purchased fertilizers, soil amendments, and other farm inputs as well.

If some of your fields are not managed organically, you must be able to show adequate buffer zones and facilities to prevent commingling of organic and conventional products. This includes a system for tracking the life cycle of everything you sell from your farm, how it was produced, and where it went. Finally, your records will enable you to develop a credible farm plan, a document central to the provisions of the Federal law. For more information on organic certification requirements, consult one of the organizations listed in appendix B.

MONITORING TILTH: READING THE FIELD

There can be wide variations within one field: differences in terrain and existing vegetation, for example. Checking for soggy areas in spring or after a good rain will reveal drainage problems. The condition of existing vegetation—whether it's weeds, forage, or field crops—can provide many clues about the status of your soil. Weeds can often be reliable indicators of potential fertility problems; the chart on page 58 lists some common weeds and the conditions they are associated with. You should also watch for signs of nutrient deficiencies, whether in weeds or cultivated crops. (Tables 7 and 8, pages 33 and 34, list some deficiency symptoms for all the important nutrients.)

You may even gain a new sense of respect for your weeds once you have learned to carefully examine them. Although shunned as unwelcome invaders by most farmers, weeds are often less damaging to established crops than supposed. They can also provide many free soil-improvement services if allowed to pave the way for your desired crops. Perennial weeds in particular are frequently deep-rooted, helping break up hardpans, aerate the subsoil, and bring up mineral nutrients from areas too deep for crop roots. Or they may act as cover crops, protecting the soil from wind and rain until the space is needed. Some plants are such reliable mineral accumulators that prospectors use them to indicate a possible source of deposits such as copper and selenium.

As you identify the weeds on your land, keep these considerations in mind:

- A few individual weeds don't mean much: look for consistent populations of the same species. The most reliable information comes from noticing several predominant species that all like similar kinds of soil conditions. For example, if you have a lot of plantains, chicory, and coltsfoot, it is a clearer indication of heavy, poorly drained soil than if just one of those species were there.

- Perennial weeds, which regrow each year, are better indicators of soil conditions than are annual weeds, which only survive one season.

- Many weeds can tolerate a wide range of conditions, but some are more specific in their requirements. Some indicate more than one factor—for instance, perennial sow-thistles and docks both indicate wet areas, but the dock prefers more acid soils, while thistles like a higher pH.

- The growth characteristics of the weed can tell as much as its presence. Vigorously growing leguminous weeds, such as clovers, are a sign that soil nitrogen is low. Stunted, yellowish weeds of other types may mean the same thing. The color of cornflowers will be blue on soils with a high pH and pink on acid soils.

Field Horsetail   **Red Sorrel**   **Lamb's-quarters**

FIGURE 11. *A Few Common Weeds. Sandy, droughty conditions are indicated by field horsetail while red sorrel is a sign of wet, acid soil. Lamb's-quarters are abundant in fertile soil, especially where manure has been applied.* (Source: Walters and Fenzauk, *An Acres U.S.A. Primer*)

Each growing season, make note in your field records of any changes in the predominant weed species.

LOOKING BENEATH THE SURFACE

The physical condition of your soil is its easiest aspect to evaluate. You don't need precise instruments to get a pretty good feel—literally—for its general tilth. Although your soil texture isn't likely to change much over time, the other tests are ones you may wish to repeat once a year or more: most are good indicators of how well your soil-improvement program is working.

Table 10

WEEDS AND SOIL CONDITIONS

Bindweed, Field: indicates hardpan or crusty surface with light sand texture.

Bracken, Eastern: indicates acid or low-lime soil, low potassium and low phosphorus.

Buttercup: indicates tilled or cultivated soil.

Buttercup, Creeping: indicates wet, poorly drained clay soil.

Campion, Bladder: indicates neutral or alkaline pH.

Chickweed: indicates tilled or cultivated soil with high fertility or humus unless weeds are pale and stunted, then fertility is low.

Chicory: indicates soil with heavy clay texture, tilled or cultivated with high fertility or humus unless weeds are pale and stunted, then fertility is low.

Cinquefoil, Silvery: indicates dry soil often with thin topsoil, acidic or low lime.

Colt's-foot: indicates heavy clay soil, waterlogged or poorly drained, acidic or low lime.

Daisy, Ox-eye: indicates waterlogged or poorly drained soil that has been neglected or uncultivated, acidic or low lime with low fertility.

Dandelion: indicates heavy clay soil, tilled or cultivated, acid or low lime especially on lawns.

Docks: indicates waterlogged or poorly drained soil, acid or low lime.

Grass, Quack: indicates hardpan or crusty surface.

Hawkweeds: indicates acidic or low-lime soil.

Henbane, Black: indicates neutral or alkaline pH.

Horsetail, Field: indicates sandy light soil, acidic or low lime.

Joe-pye Weed: indicates wet or waterlogged soil.

Knapweeds: indicates acidic or low-lime soil with high potassium.

Knotweed, Prostrate: indicates tilled or cultivated soil, acidic or low lime.

Lamb's-quarters: indicates tilled or cultivated soil with high fertility or humus unless weeds are pale and stunted, then fertility is low.

Lettuce, Prickly: indicates tilled or cultivated soil.

Meadowsweet, Broad-leaved: indicates wet or waterlogged soil.

Mosses: indicates waterlogged or poorly drained soil, acidic or low lime.

Mullein, Common: indicates neglected uncultivated soil, acidic or low lime, low fertility.

Mustards: indicates hardpan or crusty surface, dry often with thin topsoil.

Mustard, White: Indicates neutral or alkaline pH.

Nettles: indicates tilled or cultivated soil, acidic or low lime.

Pigweed, Redroot: indicates tilled or cultivated soil, high fertility or humus unless weeds are pale or stunted, which indicates low fertility.

Pineappleweed: indicates hardpan or crusty surface.

Plantains: indicates heavy clay soil, waterlogged or poorly drained, tilled or cultivated, acidic or low lime especially on lawns.

Shepherd's Purse: indicates saline soil.

Sorrel, Garden: indicates waterlogged or poorly drained soil, acidic or low lime.

Sorrel, Sheep: indicates sandy light soil, acidic or low lime.

Sow-thistle, Annual: indicates heavy clay soil.

Sow-thistle, Perennial: indicates wet soil, neutral or alkaline pH.

Stinkweed: indicates hardpan or crusty surface, high lime.

Thistle, Canada: indicates heavy clay soil.

Yarrow: indicates low potassium.

SOURCE: Hill and Ramsey, "Weeds as Indicators of Soil Conditions." *Tilth*, Summer, 1975, pp. 21–25

Texture

Your soil's texture is a key factor in how well it can hold water and nutrients, and allow air to circulate. You can evaluate the texture by scooping up a handful of moist soil—adding a little water if it's very dry—and squeezing it in your fist. Now open your hand; if your sample falls apart instead of staying in a ball, you've got sand on your hands. If you have a ball of soil sitting on your palm, try to squeeze it upward with your thumb to form a ribbon. Make as long a ribbon as you can, and measure it. If you could make a ball but not a ribbon, classify your soil as loamy sand.

Now add water to your ribbon to make a soupy mud in your hand. Rub the forefinger of your other hand in it, and decide if it feels mostly smooth, mostly gritty, or equally smooth and gritty. Then match up your observations with the length of the ribbon you made on the chart below to find the texture that most describes your soil.

Table 11

SOIL CLASSIFICATION TEST

	Feels mostly gritty	*Feels mostly smooth*	*Feels both gritty & smooth*
Forms ribbon shorter than 1"	Sandy Loam	Silty Loam	Loam
Forms ribbon 1"–2"	Sandy Clay Loam	Silty Clay Loam	Silty Clay
Forms ribbon longer than 2"	Sandy Clay	Silty Clay	Clay

SOURCE: Adapted from Sarratonio, *Methodologies for Screening Soil-Improving Legumes.*

Moisture

Once you know your soil's texture, you can more precisely determine how moist it is. Check moisture levels early in the growing season and any time you are concerned about the availability of water for your crops. Plants will wilt if soil moisture in their root zone drops below a range of 5 percent for sandy soils to 15 percent for clay soils. If soil moisture levels, as determined by the following method, are not above the 50 percent range within a six-inch depth, many crops will suffer from lack of water. If your soil dries out to less than 50 percent moisture at this depth two days after a good rain, your soil is excessively drained.

First, look for obvious signs of surface crusting and cracking caused by dryness. See how far down you have to dig before the soil gets darker, indicating more moisture. Take handfuls of soil from different depths and squeeze them firmly in your hand. If your hand gets wet, your soil is saturated. Using the chart on page 61, match the behavior of your handful of soil with the appropriate texture and description to see how much water it contains.

Drainage

A simple perc test will tell you if you have drainage problems. Dig a hole about a foot deep and six inches across. Now fill it with water and allow it to drain completely. As soon as it does, fill it again and see how long it takes to drain again. If it takes more than eight hours, you should make drainage a top priority.

The rate at which water will infiltrate soil is a useful indicator of its porosity, and can be monitored with a free and easy on-farm test. The only tools required are a one-quart Mason jar, a tape measure, and a watch that can time seconds. In a representative part of the field, at a time when the soil is neither particularly wet nor particularly dry, empty the quart of water at soil level and start counting seconds. When the water has completely soaked into the ground, stop counting

Table 12

GUIDE FOR JUDGING SOIL MOISTURE

FEEL OR APPEARANCE OF SOIL

Available Soil Moisture Remaining	Light Texture	Medium Texture	Heavy Texture
0 to 25 percent	Dry, loose, flows through fingers.	Powdery dry, sometimes slightly crusted but easily broken down into into powdery condition.	Hard, baked, cracked, sometimes has loose crumbs on surface.
25 to 50 percent	Appears to be dry, will not form a ball.*	Somewhat crumbly but holds together under pressure.	Somewhat pliable, will ball under pressure.*
50 to 75 percent	Tends to ball under pressure, but seldom holds together.	Forms a ball somewhat plastic, will sometimes slick slightly with pressure.	Forms a ball, ribbons out between thumb and forefinger.
75 percent to field capacity (100 percent)	Forms weak ball, breaks easily, will not slick.	Forms a ball, is very pliable, slicks readily if relatively high in clay.	Easily ribbons out between fingers, has slick feeling.
At field capacity (100 percent)	Upon squeezing, no free water appears on soil, but wet outline of ball is left on hand.	Upon squeezing, no free water appears on soil, but wet outline of ball is left on hand.	Upon squeezing, no free water appears on soil, but wet outline of ball is left on hand.
Saturated	Water appears on ball and hand.	Water appears on ball and hand.	Water appears on ball and hand.

*Ball is formed by squeezing a handful of soil very firmly.

SOURCE: Soil Conservation Service, *Information Bulletin No. 199* seconds and measure the diameter of the wet spot. Multiply the diameter by the number of seconds required for the water to soak in, and write the number in your field notebook or field records.

For the purposes of this test it doesn't matter whether measurements are in inches or metric units, and farmers with clayey soils may prefer to use only a pint of water. What is important is that the volume of water is the same every time. If the soil is tested this way three or four times each summer and the results averaged, it will be possible to track subtle changes over the years. Declining numbers indicate the soil's improving ability to absorb water, reduce erosion, and so on. Increasing numbers suggest that the system is deteriorating. Averages can be roughly compared from field to field (within the same soil type), but not from farm to farm.

Structural Soundness

The size of the crumbs or aggregates that make up your soil, and how well they hold together, is a critical aspect of its tilth. The bigger the crumbs, the bigger the pore spaces between them, and the better water and air can infiltrate. Soils with good structure can hold up to twice as much water as those with poor structure and the same texture. Plants grow better in soils with good structure, even when water isn't a problem.

First, simply pick up a handful of soil and see how it crumbles. Heavy soils with good structure will still crumble easily, and light soils will retain some shape instead of becoming powdery. Heavy soils with poor structure will resist crumbling or form large clods, while lighter soils will become dusty.

Next, dig a hole about a foot deep and examine the size of the crumbs at different depths. Look for large crumbs, about $\frac{1}{32}$ to $\frac{3}{8}$ inch in size. Check aggregate stability by placing a small handful of soil in a glass and filling it with water. Do the aggregates keep their shape, or does your sample collapse into a muddy blob? Good structure is indicated by a lot of large crumbs that hold together in a glass of water.

Compaction

Compaction problems can be indicated by poor water infiltration, as shown by your perc test, as well as by poor structure. If you can't plunge a garden fork into your soil to its full depth without standing on it, assuming you haven't hit a rock or other obstacle, your soil is compacted. Another way to judge compaction is to shove a thin ($\frac{1}{4}$-inch) metal rod into the ground as far as it will go until it bends under pressure. Try this in various locations: the sooner it bends, the more compacted the soil. A more precise reading of compaction can be taken with a simple hand-held tool called a penetrometer.

Scientific evaluation of soil compaction is measured by three criteria: **bulk density** tells you the weight of a given volume of soil, **pore space** indicates the proportion of a given volume of soil taken up by air and water, and **oxygen diffusion rate** measures how readily air passes through soil (see table 4, page 20). You can measure your soil's bulk density yourself, by following the instructions (below).

Digging Deeper

To get a real worm's-eye view of your soil, you might feel inspired to dig down a bit farther—two or three feet. If you have some project that entails digging a hole anyway, take a few minutes to make the following observations:

- Examine the layers of soil you see, and try to identify different horizons. The thickness and nature of each soil horizon tells a story about how the soil was formed, its drainage characteristics, and biological and chemical activity. The soil classification scheme described on pages 10–11 is based on characteristic features of different soil profiles. How thick is the topsoil? Are there sharply delineated layers below, with differences in color and/or texture? Mottled gray and rust brown streaks in lower horizons indicate leached, acid soils and possible drainage problems. Brown and red colors are from oxidized iron, a result of acidity. Absence of definite horizons may indicate very deep topsoil, a muck or organic soil, or a young soil that has not been subject to a long weathering process. Layers of different colored clays are commonly found in tropical soils.

- How deeply do plant roots penetrate? How far down do you find worm tunnels and castings, or other visible creatures?

- Note the depth of any compacted layer or hardpan, where roots end abruptly.

- Note the depth of any area of bedrock, gravel, or other kind of stone.

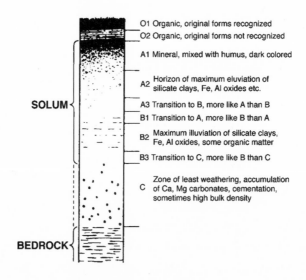

FIGURE 12. *Soil Horizons. "O" layers are topsoil; "A," "B," and "C" layers are subsoil. It is sometimes easy to see clear differentiation between horizons. In spodosols (characteristic of the Northeast), there are distinct color changes where minerals are leached from the "A2" horizon are precipitated in the "B2" horizon.*

Reprinted with permission of MacMillan Publishing Company from *The Nature and Properties of Soils*, 8th Ed., by Nyle C. Brady. Copyright 1974 by MacMillan Publishing Company.

A key component of soil vitality is the movement of water, soil life, organic matter, and nutrients between the topsoil and the subsoil. The nature of the topsoil-subsoil boundary is a wonderful indirect test that summarizes multiple factors.

If the topsoil is largely uncoupled from the subsoil, the boundary between the two will be distinctly visible, and relatively even. Very little organic matter or microbial activity crosses such a barrier, which is usually caused by cultivation methods. In a vital soil, by comparison, the topsoil-subsoil boundary is quite uneven and fairly gradual. Roots penetrate to greater depth, and when they decay they leave darker channels that couple the topsoil to the subsoil.

Once you've caught the soil exploration bug, you may want to pursue a few more sophisticated observations. The following measurements require simple tools, and in some cases involve waiting awhile to see the results.

Erosion Watch

If you are concerned about soil loss on a slope, there are a couple of methods that can confirm that erosion is taking place. The first involves driving a hollow cylinder into the soil—a six-inch piece of plastic sewer pipe works well—so that the soil level inside the cylinder is the same as that outside. Place it on the upper end of the plot in question. Cover the cylinder and check it periodically. If the soil level outside gets lower than that inside, you will know that soil is being lost.

The second method involves sinking a pie pan into the soil anywhere on the slope. Angle it in line with the slope, and make the lip level with the soil surface. Check after a heavy rain to see if you have caught some runaway soil in your pan.

Bulk Density

Although considered a technical observation, periodic monitoring of bulk density is one of the most conclusive indicators of changes in soil tilth. It isn't hard to measure: choose a spot that is relatively undisturbed, and start by scraping away the surface to level it a bit. Then dig a hole about six inches deep and four inches in diameter, saving all the soil you take out in a bag, and smooth out the bottom of the hole.

Now stuff a plastic bag into the hole and fill it up with a measured amount of water: use a kitchen measuring cup to dip it out of a bucket. Be sure the water is as close as possible to the soil surface, and record the total volume of water it took to fill the hole (use metric units to be able to compare the figures with scientific data). This figure gives you the volume of soil you removed.

Next you have to dry the soil by spreading it on a cookie sheet in the oven with the setting left on "Warm" for a day or so. Then weigh it. If you are using metric figures, you will need a scale that reads in grams. You can now calculate the bulk density (B.D.) by dividing the weight of the soil by the volume. A good range is 1.0 to 1.8 grams per cubic centimeter. More than 2.0 grams per cubic centimeter is a sign of compaction.

Field Capacity

Field capacity is a measure of how much water your soil can hold when it is saturated—increasing field capacity is another sign of increased humus content. Perform this test a day or two after a soaking rain, or you can flood a small area first; if you do, wait until the water has soaked down into the lower levels. Now dig up a few samples of soil from areas two to four inches deep—an ounce or two is enough.

Weigh the sample you collected, then dry it in the same way as described for bulk density, above. Then weigh the dry soil, making sure to subtract the weight of the container it is in each time.

The figure for field capacity is expressed as a percentage, calculated as:

$$\frac{\text{wet weight of soil} - \text{dry weight of soil}}{\text{dry weight of soil}} \times 100\% = \text{Field Capacity}$$

For comparison, well-granulated silt loam has a field capacity of about 15 percent.

EVALUATING BIOLOGICAL HEALTH: LOOKING AT LIFE FORMS

Any time you work in the soil, you should be noticing how biologically active it is. Try to identify the kinds of macroorganisms you see crawling, skittering, and squirming around as you transplant or hand-weed. An inexpensive hand lens can open up a whole universe of creatures you never knew existed.

Organic Content

There are also more pointed observations you can make, to evaluate a potential garden site or to track improvements in your soil's biological activity. It's a good idea to have organic matter content measured when you have your soil tested (see page 75–76), but you can visually evaluate it yourself. In general, darker browns mean higher humus content. Look for the white threads of fungal mycelia and bits of undecomposed organic matter. If your soil is biologically active, you will not be able to recognize crop residues from the previous season within a few weeks of spring planting. However, if you still find old cornstalks and broccoli stems in June, or a layer of sod from last fall's tillage, you need to work on stimulating soil organisms.

Counting on Worms

An "earthworm census" is a valuable barometer of soil biological activity and overall system health. When you count your worms, be sure to avoid examining places that would distort the results, such as near a compost pile or under mulch. Also, do this during a cool time of day, to avoid exposing worms to harmful conditions. Use any of these methods for estimating the earthworm population of your soil. Record your earthworm estimates several times per season, and use the season average to gauge changes in soil health from year to year.

- Measure out a one-foot-square plot and dig down six inches, placing everything you dig up in a bucket or pan. You should find at least ten earthworms in that much good, healthy soil.

- Take a "spade-split" of soil, about two inches thick and eight inches deep. Each earthworm in the spade-split represents about 100,000 worms per acre. Take several spade-splits per field, and record the average estimated earthworm population.

- Simply count the number of earthworm holes, with their little piles of castings next to them, observable in the same well-delineated area over the course of a season, and compare that number from year to year.

Rooting for Healthy Soil

The condition of plant roots is one of the ultimate indicators of soil health. Observe the root systems of weeds as you pull them up. You can also dig up a plant just to examine its roots, being careful to cut off as little as possible of its root mass. Choose the healthiest-looking specimen in the vicinity, and try to answer the following questions:

- Do the roots seem vigorous and well branched? You want to see roots penetrating as much of the soil area as possible: track the approximate volume and depth of root mass in a given area as an indicator of changes in biological health.

- Are there lots of fine root hairs? Finding only a few fine feeder roots might indicate that too little air is available in the root zone.

- Do roots grow freely in every direction, or do they seem to grow sideways at a certain depth? Roots which suddenly turn sideways are a sure indication of a hardpan.

The root systems of legumes, such as clover, vetch, and garden beans, should contain a good sprinkling of nodules. This is where the nitrogen-fixing rhizobia bacteria live. If you slice open some of these nodules, they should be noticeably pink or red in color. A green or black color indicates a lack of bacterial activity. (This may be a normal phase, however, if the plant is entering dormancy.) The size and number of nodules is directly related to how much nitrogen the plant can fix. Different species of legumes normally differ as to rates of nodulation; alfalfa and clover are generally more heavily nodulated than beans or peas. Using the right bacterial inoculants on your legume crops will increase nodulation.

Regular observation and recording of as much information as possible about your soil's physical and biological condition, in addition to your records of crop health and yields, will give you a solid basis for evaluating the progress of your fertility improvement program. This, combined with chemical analysis of soil nutrient content, will help you achieve optimum soil health and crop productivity.

Soil Nutrient Testing

Much of the soil testing in ecological farming should be focused on monitoring the vitality of the whole system and its components. Soil nutrient testing is simply one component of the farm management and decision-making process. In particular, it is a means of monitoring conditions and progress toward a goal.

The accuracy of the soil test and resultant recommendations depend on many factors including: sampling procedure, analytical process, and laboratory "philosophy" in interpreting the results. If these factors are fully understood the soil test can be a useful, if limited, guide to ecological soil management.

A farmer or gardener has three soil-testing choices: a home test kit, a government or university test, or a private laboratory. Those with a natural scientific curiosity may be well served by the purchase of a soil test kit. Useful kits range in price from $45 to $150. These kits will measure nitrogen, phosphorus, potassium, pH, and often organic matter, calcium, and magnesium. The chemical reagents and simplified procedure normally allow "ballpark" accuracy, though cheaper kits may lead to misleading results.

University or government tests tend to be limited in scope, but are often backed by "field response" data (see figure 13). This research correlates yield differences with fertilizer applications for specific soil types and test results. The resulting data are used as a basis for fertilizer recommendations. Some private labs, such as A & L Agricultural Laboratories, offer more elaborate tests, such as base saturation ratios, cation exchange capacity, and quantified results (as compared to "high, medium, low"). These soil audits are more expensive than university tests. (Figure 14 is an example.)

FIGURE 13. *Field Response Data Illustrated. Each dot represents a field test plot. The distribution of responses shows a greater response to higher soil phosphorus by potatoes than by wheat.*

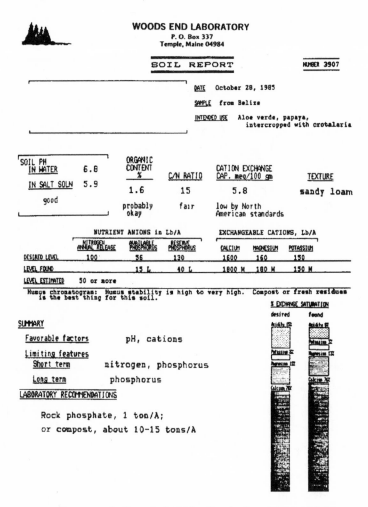

FIGURE 14. *Sample Soil Test Results for a Tropical Soil.*

Testing Procedure

Soil sampling procedures are often the most important part of soil testing. Ironically, they are also the area of greatest weakness. Sampling information is available from any private or public soil testing lab. Take all recommendations about getting a representative sample seriously; a surface sample from only a small area of a field will be misleading.

Even a carefully taken sample is not an accurate picture of actual field conditions. Chemical reagents do not interact with soil the same way that plants do. Your sample is only to plow depth, whereas deeper levels of soil can provide significant nutrients. Moreover, soil chemistry can be quite different at different times of year and moisture conditions, and may even vary from day to day. For example, researchers at the University of Vermont have found significant differences between the reactions of soils that are dried prior to testing and those that are tested moist. This perspective should be considered whenever you use soil testing to make management decisions.

The calculations that appear on laboratory report forms look impressively precise, but the degree to which those numbers represent conditions in your soil can range from "pretty good" to "anybody's guess." The analytical procedures used in labs vary enormously. Some chemical reagents and procedures are appropriate for certain soil conditions but not for others. In addition, in order to keep costs low, some labs sacrifice analytical precision by using less expensive equipment or less labor-intensive methods. Various errors, both human and computer, can also occur. There is also a lack of standardization or inter-lab agreement about soil testing procedures in general.

Fertilizer Recommendations

There are no universal standards for optimum mineral levels for all soil and crop situations. A representative sample—analyzed by appropriate testing methods, yielding accurate numbers—can still bring different fertilizer recommendations from different labs. Some labs accept certain standards for sufficient level of available nutrients (S.L.A.N.). Others recommend higher levels for "maintenance" of minerals, while many private laboratories use the Albrecht formula of base cation saturation ratio (B.C.S.R.). Often these methods are combined for different nutrients or soils. Regardless of philosophy, labs base their interpretations on their experience with previous recommendations.

The value of soil tests will depend on continued research, which considers the effect of different fertilizer rates, not just on yield, but on crop nutritional quality. In some schools of thought, less emphasis is placed on soil testing. The biodynamic view stresses humus quality over mineralization. Others maintain that plant feeding is more dependent on energy flows than the level of soluble minerals in the soil.

Soil testing is a useful management tool for the farmer, in spite of its limitations. Regular soil test results from the same lab, sampled at the same time of year, can be compared with field information from year to year. This information is a valuable gauge of progress in soil fertility management.

Interpreting Your Test Results

How closely should you follow the information given in soil tests? Read the fertilizer recommendations and explanatory notes carefully, and compare them to nutrient levels discovered. Some lab reports simply tell you how much nitrogen, phosphorus, potassium, and magnesium you need per acre, leaving the choice of fertilizer to your discretion. Services that tell you the actual versus desired level of nutrients allow you to check fertilizer recommendations for arithmetical errors. If you don't understand why any recommendation is made, contact the testing service. Recommendations are often based on your intentions for the field: if you change your plans, nutrient requirements may change as well. (Further details about fertilizer use and availability are given in chapter 4.)

Cation Exchange Capacity and pH: Both of these figures indicate how effectively your soil is able to store nutrients and release them to plants. Both are fairly accurate, but pH values can vary by about half a unit, depending on whether the test is done in water or salt solution. Recommendations should be aimed at attaining a pH of about 6.5 for general purposes.

Other than adding lots of organic matter, there is little that can be done to significantly alter the cation exchange capacity. But the CEC does have a bearing on how much fertilizer you'll need. If the soil's CEC is derived mainly from its organic matter rather than its clay content, raising a low pH can improve the CEC as well. For every increase in the CEC, more cations (generally calcium in lime) will be required to raise the pH the same amount. If you have a high cation exchange capacity but depleted mineral reserves, more fertilizer is needed to satisfy crops, since the soil reserves will keep some of the cations unavailable to crop roots.

Major Cation Nutrients: Testing procedures for calcium, magnesium, and potassium are quite accurate, and the results are reliable indicators of soil needs. Private labs subscribing to the Albrecht formula (see page 35) will indicate relationships between these elements and acidity (percent base saturation). This will tell you whether general nutrient levels need to be increased across the board, or whether one element in particular is lower than the others.

The best practice is to first bring all nutrients into balance, and then increase their overall levels—up to the optimum desired— while keeping the pH around 6.5. You can do this by looking up the analysis of the fertilizer you plan to use and multiplying the percentage of a given component by the number of pounds you will apply per acre. Then compare the result with the difference between desired and actual levels shown for that nutrient. For example, if you are using Sul-Po-Mag (which contains about 22 percent K_2, 18 percent MgO, and 22 percent SO_4) and want to add about one hundred pounds of potash per acre, you should use approximately five hundred pounds of Sul-Po-Mag per acre. However, you would also be adding about fifty pounds of magnesium (in the form of MgO) per acre, so you would want to make sure that this won't send your potassium:magnesium balance out of whack.

CALCULATING CATION FERTILIZER NEEDS

Laboratory recommendations for cation fertilizers are given in pounds per acre. The chemistry upon which those recommendations are based depends on the valence of the element in question, not its weight. Valence refers to the charge of an ion and the number of electrons it accepts or gives up when forming a neutral bond.

Of the major cations, calcium (Ca^{2+}) and magnesium (Mg^{2+}) occupy the same number of cation exchange sites, though calcium weighs a little more than magnesium (by a factor of 1.2). Therefore, you need fewer pounds of magnesium than of calcium to neutralize acid conditions. In other words, when considering the need for a good soil cation balance, you should expect to find about ten times as much calcium as magnesium *by weight* in test results. This corresponds to a base saturation ratio of six or seven to one.

Potassium (K^+) has only half the chemical charge of calcium or magnesium, and so requires twice as many ions to fill the same number of cation exchange sites. One ion of potassium, moreover, weighs a good deal more than one of magnesium. Therefore, although magnesium occupies three to four times the number of soil cation exchange sites as potassium, it is required in less than twice the amount of potassium by weight in your soil.

Organic Matter and Nitrogen: The quality of organic matter—that is, its balance between fresh, decomposing forms and stable humus—is more indicative of soil health than its quantity. Monitoring organic matter quality is less of a science than an art, one that is developed through observation and experience. Measuring organic matter quantity can nevertheless be of value for comparing changes over time in the same field, especially when combined with observations of soil structure, porosity, and water-holding capacity.

Several cautions are in order. Readings of organic matter quantity may vary considerably, depending on which test is used. One common test is combustion, in which a dry soil sample is weighed, burned, and weighed again. The difference is assumed to be organic matter. There are also several chemical digestion methods, and some tests that supposedly measure humus. Make sure that the testing methods are the same before trying to compare results. Similarly, organic matter is usually highly variable within a field, making consistent sampling procedures very important.

Nitrogen is considered the least reliable of chemical tests because of fluctuations in soil nitrogen levels and availability. Some labs simply estimate nitrogen at about 5 percent of organic matter, which can vary as noted above. For these reasons, many labs do not test for nitrogen, although a test developed by the University of Vermont has proven to be more accurate.

Nitrogen recommendations are generally based on crop need, rather than existing reserves in the soil. You must take into account field history factors such as: contributions from leguminous crops and green manures, varying nitrogen uptake of preceding crops, and previous applications of manures and other organic matter.

Annual nitrogen release (mineralization) can be estimated by considering humus stability, along with total organic matter content and average annual temperature for your region (which influences the rate of microbial activity). Improving the level of organic matter will improve soil productivity. Proper management of organic matter is a never-ending necessity—no matter how positive your test results are.

Energy cycle: Organic matter is stored solar energy. Testing soil organic matter quality can provide an indirect evaluation of how well the farm system is capturing and storing solar energy, since when the energy cycle is functioning well, soil organic matter contains a balance of fresh, decomposing, and stable organic matter.

Organic matter *quantity* is less indicative of soil health, as it is largely dependent on soil drainage and average annual temperature.

Most farm activities tend to decrease organic matter levels from what they would naturally be under sod or forest conditions. Cool climates and imperfectly drained soils each tend to favor higher levels of soil organic matter, making direct comparisons from region to region difficult, and emphasizing once again the importance of following the long-term trends for each field.

Except for occasional testing to ensure that organic matter levels are not declining over the years, measuring the quantity of soil organic matter is probably not as effective a management tool as some of the indirect tests used to evaluate the water cycle.

Phosphate: Phosphate is another complex nutrient: it is uncertain how accurately testing procedures reflect growing conditions and the variety of factors influencing phosphate availability. Again, the numbers appearing in soil test results shouldn't be too heavily relied upon for calculating fertilizer needs. Since ecological practices stress building reserves that are made available gradually through organic matter decomposition, you are quite safe in applying as much rock or colloidal phosphate as you can afford if the phosphate level tests low.

If organic matter content is low, using fish emulsion to "water in" transplants, or for foliar feeding (see chapter 4) will boost available phosphate. Acidulated phosphate fertilizers respond to immediate crop demands rather than building the soil. Of course, the pH and organic matter content of your soil strongly influence the availability of reserve or applied phosphate to plants, and are therefore just as important as measured soil phosphate levels in ensuring adequate phosphate levels for crops.

Minor and Trace Elements: In general, as the level of an element declines in a sample, testing procedures become more expensive and less reliable. Plant tissue tests are a better means of evaluating micronutrient nutrition. Tests are readily available for sulfur, boron, copper, manganese, zinc, and iron; of these, the most extensively researched is for boron. Such tests are most valuable when you plan to grow a crop with a high demand for some specific minor element (such as boron for alfalfa or brassicas), or have cause to suspect a deficiency. In the case of a deficiency, use micronutrient supplements with extreme caution to avoid undermining crucial balances.

Soil "Hazards": Some soil tests also indicate the level of exchangeable aluminum ions, which is often excessive in the northeastern U.S. Under conditions of low pH, aluminum becomes more available—a problem because of its toxicity to plants and the fact that it interferes with the availability of nutrients like phosphate. Raising the pH by liming eliminates the hazard. It is also possible to have your soil tested for toxic heavy metals, such as lead, cadmium, selenium, and mercury. Check with your nearest university soil lab to find out how.

If the farm has a recent history of using agricultural chemicals, then testing soil, plants, and water for residues of these chemicals may be an important means of monitoring how well the farm system is beginning to "clean itself out." If the farm has been in hay for the last twenty years, residue testing is probably less important, but it should be remembered that some of the early pest control products (such as lead arsenate and DDT) leave significant residues for decades. Because both residue sampling and testing are complicated (and therefore expensive) procedures, competent professional assistance is usually advisable.

Tissue Analysis and Other Tests

By complementing a soil test with a tissue (usually leaf or petiole) analysis, a more complete picture of soil fertility emerges. Parameters for nutrient levels in many plants, at different growth stages, have been established. Plant root systems draw nutrients from a large area of the topsoil and subsoil. Plant tissue analysis reveals a lot about levels of soil nutrients, as well as that plant's ability to obtain them. It is important that the tissue sample is taken from the correct areas of the plant and at a growth stage for which parameters are established.

Crops are often tested after harvest for nutrient and energy content. This information is generally used for balancing livestock feed rations. However, it also indicates how available soil nutrients are to crops—another indicator of soil fertility.

Some agricultural consultants also test the plant's nutrient status with a **refractometer,** a hand-held instrument that measures the sugar content of cell sap. Sugar content is closely related to plant mineral content. By placing a few drops of sap on a glass plate at one end, a visual display tells the percent of sugar content according to the **Brix scale.** An experienced consultant can estimate plant and soil health by comparing the results to established parameters.

Soil tests, tissue analysis, indicator weeds, test strips, and refractometer checks are among the tools available to give you feedback about your own observations of soil health. Many other innovative testing techniques are also available for the farmer interested in exploring the frontiers of farm system monitoring. These are frequently discussed in publications such as *Acres U.S.A.,* and may assist the monitoring and evaluation process considerably.

The important thing to remember about soil testing is that it involves far more than laboratory analysis. Laboratory work is a useful supplement to the more important on-farm testing and observation, but lab results alone are of limited utility for a management system that attempts to do more than achieve simple target yields.

When coupled with sound and holistic farm management, thoughtful monitoring to learn how clean, vital, and diverse the farm system is, will contribute significantly to making the farm happy, healthy, and prosperous.

4

SOIL MANAGEMENT
PRACTICES

Once you have evaluated your soil's ferility needs you can begin putting some ecological management methods into practice.

This chapter will describe the techniques that you can use to improve the physical qualities of your soil, build its organic matter and humus content, and choose the most suitable off-farm sources of nutrients.

MANAGING PHYSICAL FACTORS: DRAINAGE, IRRIGATION, TILLAGE, AND CULTIVATION

In planning the most appropriate soil management practices the first factor to consider is soil moisture and soil aeration. The most sophisticated fertilization program will give scant return if the soil does not have a proper moisture/air balance. This balance will not be present if the land is poorly drained or does not have adequate moisture. Organic farming relies on conventional drainage practices if these are ecologically sound, complying with marshland conservation measures. Organic management in arid areas can even drought-proof soil to some extent. Tillage practices will vary depending on the soil and climate, but the principle is to preserve organic matter in the top horizon. In situations where perennial crops are being raised, perma-cultural practices largely replace annual tillage and most cultivation. Organic farmers have been the leaders in developing innovative me-chanical cultivation systems for weed control, but that only serves to supplement control based on a well-tuned crop rotation.

Drainage

Farming in areas where the water table is high may require subter-ranean tiling with perforated pipe or a gridwork of ditches. Heavy clay soils and those with subsoil hardpan layers may require special measures, such as subsoiling with a bulldozer, to allow better water and root penetration. Many soils that drain poorly simply require ecological management to improve percolation and break up plow pans and compaction, but structural problems may require drainage. Consult your Extension or Soil Conservation Service for the most appropriate local services.

Irrigation

It is not within the scope of this book to discuss the ecological ethics or practical implementation of irrigation in organic farming systems. Suffice it to say that if irrigation is appropriate on any farm it should be managed so that water use is optimized. In practice that would mean that flood irrigation would not be as acceptable as drip irriga-tion. The principle of ecological management is to improve the water-retention capability of soils and design the farming system to optimize the water cycle. This is accomplished in arid areas by following guid-ance offered in systems such as permaculture, holistic management or keyline management, not in rerouting rivers to desert areas.

Tillage

The function of tillage is to incorporate organic matter and mineral fertilizers into the soil, aerate the soil, improve water permeability, control weeds, and prepare a seedbed. Since all tillage destroys organic matter and causes compaction to some degree, tillage systems should be designed for minimal use and damage to soil structure.

A tillage system should work crop residues and other organic matter into the topsoil, where, in the presence of bacteria and other life forms, it can be digested. Some sort of vegetative cover or litter should be left on the soil during the northern winter, southern dry season, or tropical rainy season. A properly managed tillage system creates a seedbed where carbon dioxide, oxygen, nitrogen, and water circulate through the soil, fostering the biological processes that create soil fertility and plant growth.

Seedbeds are often created in a way that damages soil structure, resulting in erosion, compaction, and organic matter oxidation. For example, one common conventional method is fall moldboard plowing, spring discing, and a final harrowing. The plow can create a hardpan with annual use, bury organic matter and living topsoil in an anaerobic zone, allow bare subsoil to erode by wind and water, and obstruct the capillary action of water. Spring discing breaks down the clumps, but it also causes compaction especially in wet conditions. The field may look good after the final harrowing, but not without great expense to soil tilth.

Properly designed tillage tools avoid these problems. Although the moldboard plow is useful to turn a heavy sod, it is inappropriate for most farms. New types of plows, such as the English paraplow, Australian keyline plow, and the German bio-plow, can accomplish plowing tasks without the detrimental effect of conventional plowing. Many organic farmers base their system on the chisel plow for deep tillage in the fall and offset discs for seedbed creation in the spring. Rotovators are used by a number of farmers, especially market gardeners. While they do mix organic matter into the top layer, they can create a hardpan and leave the soil too fluffy. They are best employed on a sandy soil, with a subsoiler or heavy chisel used annually to break up the hardpan.

In response to tillage problems, and in recognition of the need to nurture a living soil, a number of combination tools such as the Lely

Roterra, Glencoe Soil Saver, Landoll Soil Master, and Weichel Terravator have been developed. These tools have their proponents and have grown in popularity since the early 1980s.

The other development in conservation tillage tools has been the Ridge Till and Zone Till systems. These tools, developed and promoted by companies like Buffalo Farm Equipment, create field ridges for overwintering and spring planting. Ridging seems to decrease erosion, create a dynamic seedbed, and allow for easy weed control. No-till systems usually rely on herbicides and hence are unsuitable for organic farming.

Ecological tillage is as much a question of timing as it is one of proper equipment. Only experience with your own soil and climatic conditions, combined with knowledge of equipment capabilities, will lead to an appropriate tillage system for your farm.

Cultivation

The main reason for cultivation is weed control. Cultivation also breaks up soil crusts and stimulates biological activity through aeration. However, at the same time it oxidizes organic matter and damages soil structure.

Weeds are a major challenge for organic farmers. Weeds are controlled but never eliminated under ecological management systems. Knowing the life cycle of problem weed species can enable you to decide on the best method of control. A well-tuned crop rotation is the basis of ecological weed control. Aspects of rotations include:

- Mixing sod and row crops in rotation, alternating control methods for warm- and cool-season weeds, and matching crop needs to nutrient levels—especially nitrogen—so that excesses do not spur weed growth.

- Green-manure smother crops like buckwheat, and allelopathic crops like rye (which excrete exudates that suppress competition).

- "Living mulches" or legume intercrops that smother weeds as well as fixing nitrogen and adding organic matter. Sometimes weeds themselves can function as a mulch if they do not set seed or spread.

- In perennial crop settings timely mowing can control weeds if shading or competition do not.

- Animal grazing, especially when optimized with movable fencing.

Biological controls, such as weed-eating insects and weed diseases, are becoming more popular as chemical companies diversify into bio-rationals and introduce ecological products. Plastic mulch of varying colors and degradability are also allowed to organic farmers with restrictions that include proper postseason cleanup.

These practices do not usually eliminate the need for some mechanical cultivation to control weeds; many farmers feel that there is no substitute for fast-moving steel. Innovative farmers and manufacturers keep developing increasingly effective equipment. One of the most popular implements for organic farmers is the rotary hoe. This is a tool bar mounted with circular steel-tipped wheels on individual springs. It is pulled at high speed over crops when they are two to three inches high and kicks out weed seedlings without harming established plants. Farmers have continued to modify this tool to their needs, some welding on heavier tips and trash guards to convert it to heavier tilling functions, others adding a second tool bar and holes to double its action and cut down on field trips.

Harrows have also been modified and put to uses other than finishing the field for planting. For example, light harrows are used to rake a field after planting (a procedure called "blind harrowing") to disrupt weed growth. Row cultivators have also undergone a radical change in design. The Bezzerides brothers developed attachments for cultivators that replaced discs and sweeps with spyder, thinner, spinner, and weeder tools that work the soil lighter and closer to the crop. Other innovative implements include the Lilliston rolling cultivator, Rau-Kombi vibra-shank, and the Lely weeder. Ridge tilling also has its own style of cultivating equipment.

There are other approaches available when fast steel isn't appropriate. The Bärtschi Company has developed an effective brush weeder whose vertically mounted polypropylene brush wheels scrub between crop rows. This tool works well in wet weather and doesn't bring up new weed seeds by penetrating the soil deeply. Thermal weed control, always popular in Germany, has become better known in North America. These liquid-petroleum-powered flamers are ecologically appropriate in many situations. In citrus groves, where plastic irrigation piping prevents mechanical and flame weeding, a hot steam applicator has proved successful in trials. Electric shock machines, once popular in western sugar beet operations, are very effective on large, laser-leveled fields. There are also weeders that use mounted rubber tires to pull out established weeds. Sod crops can also be helped by mowing, harrowing, and aerating operations.

All organic weed-control methods, however, are based on timing and a healthy soil. The entire tillage system has to be timed to give the crop a competitive advantage over weeds. Some farmers eliminate fall tillage and/or delay spring tillage to plant when temperature and moisture are ideal for the quick germination and growth of crops. A healthy soil is not as prone to serious weed problems and provides a granular seedbed that ensures the rapid emergence and vigorous early growth of the crop.

ORGANIC MATTER AND HUMUS MANAGEMENT

The proper care and feeding of soil organisms demands close attention to managing soil ogranic matter. What follows is a basic overview of how to go about it.

Building and Maintaining Humus

The most important task of any ecological soil management program is creating and maintaining humus. This is not to say that other concerns, such as mineral nutrient levels, should be neglected. However, while it is possible to promote healthy soil by carefully managing organic matter and humus with little regard for balancing minerals, the reverse is rarely true.

The conventional and ecological approaches to agriculture both consider organic matter important for soil fertility, although they assign a different priority to it. But organic matter in itself is not enough. It must be continually undergoing biological transformation into stable humus. This process is entirely dependent on a healthy microbial population.

The optimal form, quantities, frequency, and timing of organic matter supplementation will be determined by environmental, management, and economic factors.

Environment: In general, warmer climates coincide with lower soil organic matter levels. Where lack of moisture isn't a limiting factor, higher temperatures cause organic matter to decompose faster than the corresponding increase in vegetative growth. Tropical soils contain little organic matter because it mineralizes as fast as it drops to the ground. In hot, dry (arid) climates, decomposition is very slow, but so is vegetative growth that would provide fresh organic matter.

Drainage and soil texture are also important. Waterlogged soil favors anaerobic decomposers over the faster aerobes. When moisture is sufficient, sandy, well-aerated soils promote faster microbial decomposition than do heavier clays, which also tend to hold onto their organic fractions more securely. Soils under grasslands in temperate climates will accumulate more organic matter than forest-covered soils of similar texture and climate zones.

Management: Sod or other permanent ground cover is the best way to protect and increase soil organic matter in temperate climates, while a polycultural design works best in the humid tropics. The more a soil is worked, the faster its organic matter will be exhausted—one reason for the promotion of minimum tillage techniques. Simply preventing erosion will eliminate one of the major causes of organic matter depletion.

Soil that suffers from compaction and poor drainage will lack the microbial populations needed to "process" organic matter; any organic matter that is added to this soil may just sit there, unavailable to crops, and with no stable humus to keep soluble nutrients from leaching away. Carefully managed cultivation techniques can keep organic matter plentiful and productive rather than exhausted or inactive.

Organic Matter and Nitrogen Availability

It is often helpful to plan organic matter management by linking it to crop nitrogen needs. (See table 13 for general crop nitrogen requirements.) Nitrogen is made available gradually as organic matter mineralizes, at a rate determined by the level of soil biological

Table 13

GENERAL CROP NITROGEN REQUIREMENTS

Crop	Pounds of nitrogen per acre per year
Grass (2–3 times as a top dressing)	100–150 (maximum)
Small grains	20–40
Potatoes	120–160
Leafy vegetables	120
Root crops	80
General home vegetables	100

NOTE: These are the guidelines used by the University of Vermont in making nitrogen fertilizer recommendations—before taking into account soil test results or past cropping history.

activity and the type of organic matter present. The addition of green manures, legumes in rotation, animal manures, and compost will supplement existing soil nitrogen levels. Carbonaceous organic matter, such as straw, sawdust, and cereal stubble will temporarily deplete soil nitrogen.

It is impossible to calculate precisely how much available nitrogen is being contributed by organic matter, but information about the amount and nature of soil organic matter, as well as the approximate rate of decomposition you can expect, can help you estimate how much of your crop's nitrogen needs can be met through organic matter. The graph below shows the relationship between available nitrogen, soil organic matter levels and annual rate of decomposition. Note that, as soil organic matter levels increase, the rate of mineralization (k) tends to decrease. Highest levels of available nitrogen occur in soils with about 3 to 4 percent organic matter, which decomposes at a rate of 3 to 4 percent per year.

The following example shows how you might estimate nitrogen availability from organic matter:

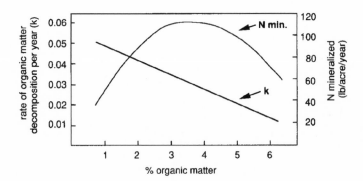

FIGURE 15: *Nitrogen availability and its relation to percent organic matter and decomposition rates.*

(Redrawn from F. R. Magdoff, *Communications in Soil Science*, 1991, p. 1512. Courtesy of Marcel Dekker, Inc., New York.)

Assume the weight of soil in the top six inches of an acre equals two million pounds. Your soil test indicates an organic matter content of 5 percent, so the weight of organic matter per acre is 100,000 pounds. Nitrogen comprises about 5 percent of organic matter, so the total nitrogen content of each acre will be 5,000 pounds. As indicated in the graph, you can reasonably expect a decomposition rate of about 2 percent a year, resulting in about 100 pounds per acre of available nitrogen from organic matter—enough for the needs of most vegetable crops.

This example also tells you how much organic matter you will need to add in order to replace what's lost through mineralization: 2 percent of 100,000 pounds, or about one ton. Some of this may come from crop residues, but additional compost, manure, or green manure in rotation will be required. You should note that this example does not account for differences in climate, moisture levels, or soil texture, all of which influence decomposition rates.

ANIMAL MANURES

Animal manure is often treated as a waste rather than an asset, particularly where the ratio of livestock to cultivated land is too high. As a result, millions of dollars worth of nitrogen, phosphorus, and potassium are discarded annually, and allowed to pollute our rivers, rather than being returned to the soil. Perhaps more important than its nutrient value, manure contributes substantially to soil organic matter and biological activity. It is rich in numbers and diversity of decomposer organisms, thus stimulating the humification process for whatever other organic materials are added to the soil.

Use of Raw Manure

Any manure that has not been left to age for at least six months, or has not been put through a composting process, is considered "raw." Raw manure, especially from poultry, is similar to synthetic nitrogen fertilizers in its effect on soil. It may also contain weed seeds, which pass unharmed through animals' digestive systems.

The application of raw manure should be avoided just before planting any produce or grain crop, and throughout the growing season. This is because it releases more nitrogen than crops need, resulting in poor quality and pest susceptibility. The excess nitrogen also increases weed growth, or is wasted. Raw manure should never be spread on snow or frozen ground: most nutrients will be lost to the crops, and will contribute to water pollution through runoff instead. There are also increasing concerns about food safety due to contamination of crops by human pathogens carried in raw manure.

The best time to spread raw manure is when it can be incorporated into the soil without delay. Some time for decomposition should be allowed before planting. As much as one-quarter of the nitrogen content can be lost due to ammonia volatilization in one day, and nearly half after four days.

In climatic zones where animals graze year-round, the use of a chain or pasture harrow is ideal to work the manure evenly into the soil.

Manure Storage

Methods of storing manure vary in cost and in the effectiveness with which they preserve nutrients. Some are well-known and accepted; others are still experimental. The right one for you depends mainly on available resources and personal inclinations.

In general, solid storage systems (such as sheltered piles) are cheaper and produce less of an unpleasant odor than liquid or slurry systems (such as lagoons). Solid storage systems require more labor to operate, but are cheaper, whereas liquid systems are costly to install but easy to manage. Some farmers have experimented with homemade aerated slurry systems, which offer the ease and convenience of liquids, but reduce odors and stabilize nutrients by aerating the contents through periodic agitation. Commercially available aerated slurry systems are currently very expensive.

Since most of the nutrient loss in manure during storage is caused by leaching, outdoor piles should ideally be covered, even if only with a layer of bedding every few days. Increasing the amount of bedding in the stall will also help retain urine, as well as improve the carbon:nitrogen ratio for more thorough decomposition. If shelter is impossible, water that runs off the pile should be channeled into a holding tank or lagoon, where it can be used (after filtering) for irrigation or to dilute foliar nutrient sprays. Many European systems have separate storage facilities for urine and runoff.

Ammonia loss from cow manure can be reduced by adding rock or colloidal phosphate to the gutter at the rate of one to two pounds per cow per day. This is also an excellent way to utilize the otherwise largely unavailable phosphate content from that source. Some farmers prefer to add it when loading the manure spreader, to avoid abrading gutter cleaning equipment.

The same guidelines for spreading raw manure apply to aged manure—especially the need to incorporate it quickly. However, well-aged manure is less likely to upset soil systems with soluble nutrients, and so can be used more safely just before planting.

COMPOSTING

Why compost? Composting is the art and science of mixing various organic materials in a pile, monitoring the resultant biological activity, and controlling conditions so that the original raw substances are transformed into a stable humus. This process of humification is a combination of biochemical degradation and microbial synthesis. Composting is a form of aerobic digestion or controlled fermentation, and differs markedly from anaerobic breakdown or putrefaction. Composting can be done on any scale—garden, farm, or industrial.

High-quality compost consists primarily of humus and offers the same benefits: it creates and supports the biological processes in the soil. Many people object to the extra time and expense necessary to make compost, asserting that the humification process takes place naturally when organic wastes are incorporated into the soil (referred to as **sheet composting**). Compost proponents counter that only composting can guarantee humus as the end product, imparting a quality rarely attained in sheet composting. Moreover, many raw materials will not readily decompose in the soil.

Very healthy soils are able to buffer the soluble portions of raw manure, break down carbonaceous materials such as sawdust, and digest such wet materials as cannery wastes; however, such soils are the exception. Compost is a microbe-laden substance that inoculates the soil, activating its biological processes. It is a source of organic matter as well as carrying a modest mineral fertilizer value.

In one study that compared compost with stockpiled feedlot manure in the Midwest, researchers found that test plots using compost resulted in yields similar to those fertilized with four times the amount of manure. In addition, measurements of soil quality (pH, organic matter levels, CEC, nitrogen, phosphorus, and potassium levels) as well as plant tissue (nitrate, phosphorus, and potassium) showed improvement on plots getting compost. These differences cannot be accounted for by the actual nutrient content of the compost, indicating that it probably improves the availability of existing soil nutrients.

Composting does involve extra time and money, but offers the following practical advantages in addition to the benefits described above:

- It stabilizes the volatile nitrogen fraction of manure by fixing it into organic forms (usually microbial bodies).

- It allows use of materials that may be toxic to soil organisms, such as cannery wastes, or that will steal soil nitrogen if applied directly to soil in the raw state, such as sawdust.

- It permits an even distribution of trace mineral soil amendments, avoiding the problem of spot imbalances.

- It eliminates most objectionable odors created by bacterial action on sulfur and nitrogen compounds.

- It reduces the volume of wastes, and therefore the number of trips to the field.

- It eliminates most pathogens and weed seeds by thermal action (when pile temperature reaches 140°F/60°C).

- The final product is easy to store and handle, and versatile in its applications.

- Recent research is proving the antifungal disease benefits of compost.

- It reduces the presence of human pathogens such as *E. coli*.

On-Farm Waste Recycling

As landfills close and tipping fees increase, composting is becoming a lucrative farm sideline, not so much from selling the finished product as a soil amendment, but as an organic waste recycling enterprise. Many municipalities are happy to deliver yard wastes and leaves directly to local farms free of charge, but frequently industrial processors, supermarkets, and other businesses will pay well for the service of hauling them away. In New Jersey, for example, one farm accepts cranberry wastes from a local plant, charging the company only one-fourth the going cost of landfilling their "waste." This translates into a substantial source of income before realizing anything from sales of the finished compost.

Before deciding to pursue industrial composting on the farm, however, keep a few warnings in mind:

- Some organic wastes can carry toxic contaminants, such as heavy metals, pesticides, or industrial by-products such as PCBs and dioxin. Some contaminants can be rendered harmless or stabilized by the composting process, but be sure to demand a laboratory analysis of any raw wastes you consider accepting. If the farm is to be certified, consult your certification agency regarding the acceptability of any off-farm wastes you want to use.

- You will probably need a permit to operate as a waste disposal site, which often presents overwhelming barriers when neighbors conjure up images of community health hazards and unpleasant smells.

- Depending on the scale, some capital investment in composting equipment (shredder, screener, and perhaps bagger) will be necessary.

- If you intend to market the finished compost, you have to be prepared to give as much attention to marketing and quality control as you would any other farm enterprise.

- Most industrial organic wastes must be mixed with some other ingredient to achieve the proper carbon:nitrogen (C:N) ratio needed for successful composting. Often this will require locating and purchasing large quantities of carbonaceous materials, since the most problematic wastes are usually high nitrogen, wet, sloppy, and smelly.

Composting Equipment and Methods

Compost-making on a garden scale has been ably described elsewhere. Optimum pile size, or critical mass, is about five feet square and four feet high, or close to two tons. The only equipment needed are manure forks and other loading tools. Many garden catalogs offer specialized compost bins, tumblers, and aerating tools in addition to shredding machines. Shredders do reduce the size of raw materials and produce more homogeneous piles, but are expensive. Rear-end rototillers can be used to turn large garden compost windrows.

Farm-scale composting requires a small tractor with a power

take-off (PTO), a PTO manure spreader, and a second tractor with a front-end loader. Most manure spreaders make good compost machines, although side-delivery types and those with unconventional beaters are not appropriate. In regions where manure spreaders are not available, front-end loaders, preferably with buckets that have long teeth, will have to be used.

The procedure is straightforward, but takes practice to master. Piles of material are arranged parallel to the projected length of the windrow. The full manure spreader begins unloading, while the front-end loader alternates between the raw material piles, dumping the proper proportion of each into the spreader. Once the pile is about four feet high and six to eight feet wide (with some hand-shaping in the early stages), the spreader is inched forward to let the raw materials hit against the new pile and fall into place. As the manure spreader slowly pulls forward, the pile is formed (see figure 17).

The manure spreader not only mixes the materials, but aerates them as it chops and throws them. This is quite different from using a front-end loader to dump (compact) materials into a windrow shape. While this is not an unnatural job for the manure spreader, it is intensive, so lots of grease and oil should be used on the chains and gears. Depending on condition of equipment and personal comfort, you can compost at any time of year. Climatic conditions will also influence the optimum pile size and ratio of materials.

Compost manufacturers, mushroom growers, research institutions, municipal sludge plants, and some farmers have developed machines specifically for compost production. These machines are designed primarily to turn piles of raw materials. Some straddle the windrow, while others turn it from the side. Turning, which controls air and moisture levels, increases the speed of composting. These machines may be equipped with tanks to spray water, which often contains bacterial inoculants. Some intermediate-scale machines, such as the "Easy Over" compost turner, can be powered by a farm tractor. Such machines could make custom composting a viable option in the near future.

Raw Materials

Anything that was once alive can be composted: it is simply a matter of creating an appropriate initial mix. Materials can be judged according to their carbon to nitrogen ratio, moisture content, and physical structure.

A reasonable carbon to nitrogen ratio for the initial mix is between 25 and 35 parts carbon to 1 part nitrogen. This ratio allows the nitrogen to "fire" the mix and decompose the carbonaceous material. A higher ratio (more carbon) will take longer to compost, slowly exhaling carbon dioxide until the proper ratio is achieved. A lower ratio results in higher nitrogen loss through volatilization or leaching.

Manure is ideal material for composting. If it must be stored for any length of time before composting, it should be mixed with bedding or litter, creating a superb base material. For example, when mixed with bedding, dairy manure has an average carbon, to nitrogen ratio of 25 to 1, although usually it is too wet. Organic materials rich in nitrogen which may be available in different areas include slaughterhouse by-products, fish wastes, leather tankage, and peanut, sugar cane, and cocoa wastes. They can be mixed with carbonaceous materials such as hay, straw, sawmill waste, vegetable wastes, bagasse, dry leaves, clippings, and rice hulls. In many tropical zones, where compost is especially valuable, many raw materials such as saw chips, sugarcane bagasse and filter-mud, rice hulls, and other wastes from large-scale export crops are readily available (see table 14 on page 98).

Nitrogenous materials are often wet, and can be balanced by drier carbonaceous wastes. If the mixture is too wet, air is excluded; too little water will not support microbial needs. The optimum initial moisture level is around 60 percent. The mix can be tested by squeezing a handful until the particles stick together. If it drips, it is too wet. If it falls apart when released, it is too dry.

Particle size and shape are also important for composting. For example, hay and straw have a lower carbon to nitrogen ratio than

FIGURE 17. *Farm Scale Composting Technique. Layout of piles of raw materials relative to windrow placement. Front-end loader alternately dumps materials into continuously operating manure spreader.*
(Drawing by Stewart Hoyt.)

sawdust, but may be less useful for composting because they absorb water only at their ends, and tend to mat, excluding air, even when put through beaters. Sawdust (actually the small chunks from a circular saw, not dust from a sander or shavings from a planer), because of its granular texture, helps form a crumb structure in a windrow when mixed with manure. This creates good aeration and an end product that is crumbly and easy to spread.

Table 14

NUTRIENT COMPOSITION OF ORGANIC MATERIALS

Listed below are approximate nutrient compositions of materials that are commonly available in the Northeast. Except for manures, informantion is provided only for nitrogen (N), Phosphate (P_2O_5) and potash (K_2O), though all of these materials contain other essential macro- and micronutrients. Carbon to nitrogen ratios are indicated for bulky materials that may be used for compost. A. High analysis organic wastes: carbon to nitrogen ratio generally 24:1 or less (often commercially available). B. N-P-K, Organic Matter, and Moisture Content of Various Manures (%) C. Carbon to nitrogen ratios of bulky organic materials.

A. PERCENT COMPOSITION

Material	*N*	*P_2O_5*	*K_2O*
Alfalfa leaf meal	3.0	0.3	0.0
Apple pomace	.20	.02	.15
Blood meal	8.0–13.0	1.5–2.0	.6–1.0
Bone meal, steamed	.70–4.0	18.0–34.0	——
Cottonseed meal	6.0	2.5–3.0	1.0–1.7
Feather meal	12.0	——	——
Fish meal	10.0	4.0–6.0	——
Hoof & horn meal	12.5	1.75	——
Leather meal	5.50–12.0	——	——
Seaweed (kelp)	0.6–0.9	0–0.5	4–13
Sewage sludge	1.5–2.0	1.4	.4–18
Sewage sludge, activated dry	2.0–6.0	3.0–7.0	0–1.0
Soybean meal	6.9–7.0	1.2–1.6	1.5–2.3
Tankage, animal	6.0–9.0	6.0–10.0	0–1.5

B. N-P-K, ORGANIC MATTER, AND MOISTURE CONTENT OF VARIOUS MANURES (%)					
Kind of Manure	Nitrogen	Phosphate	Potash	Organic Matter	Moisture
Rabbit	2.4	1.40	0.6	33	43
Chicken	1.1	0.80	0.5	25–45	55–7
Sheep	0.7	0.30	0.9	32–34	66–6
Horse	0.7	0.30	0.6	22–26	74–7
Steer	0.7	0.30	0.4	17	83
Cattle	0.6	.02	0.5	17	83
Duck	0.6	1.40	0.5	25–45	55–75
Pig	0.5	0.30	0.5	14	86

C. CARBON TO NITROGEN RATIOS OF BULKY ORGANIC MATERIALS.	
Material	Ratio
Vegetable wastes	12:1
Alfalfa hay	13:1
Seaweed	19.1
Rotted manure	20:1
Apple pomace	21:1
Legume shells (peas, soybeans, etc.)	30:1
Leaves	40–80:1
Sugarcane trash	50:1
Cornstalks	60:1
Oat straw	74:1
Chaff and hulls (various grains)	80:1
Straw	80:1
Timothy hay	80:1
Paper	170:1
Sugarcane fiber (bagasse)	200:1
Sawdust	400:1

Rock powders such as rock or colloidal phosphate, granite dust, and basalt meal can be added to the mix. They aid microbial growth in the pile, and the composting process makes them more available to plants. Lime should not be mixed with raw manure, as it liberates ammonia. Conventional soluble fertilizers tend to inhibit microbial processes, and should be avoided. Do not use sewage sludge and night soil in composts intended for use on land that produces on human food crops, because of possible contamination from human disease pathogens and heavy metals. Such materials can, however, be used in composts for shelter belts and on other nonfood crops, and possibly on green manure and forage crops. Soil is a valuable addition to initial mixes, often contributing around 2 to 5 percent of the content when scooped up with the raw materials. It also helps inoculate the pile with "native" microorganisms. For best results, use a wide variety of materials, including animal manures.

There are many compost activators on the market. Those with dormant bacterial spores are useful for composts made without cow manure or other materials rich in microbial life. Some so-called compost activators consist mainly of nitrogen fertilizers. Biodynamic preparations are not activators, per se, but specific aids and regulators of the humus-plant-cosmos energy flow.

Monitoring and Analysis

The activity of a compost pile can be divided into a breakdown and buildup phase. The microbial activity begins in a new pile almost immediately. As the microbe population explodes, it generates heat. Within three to five days the pile will reach a temperature peak of 115° to 130°F (45° to 55°C). The pile should not be allowed to exceed 140°F (60°C), as mineralization will occur. As it slowly cools, the organic matter broken down by one group of organisms is transformed into humus by another group. When composting is complete, the original mass of raw materials will be reduced by about half, the rest having been transformed into carbon dioxide by microbes.

Table 15

TROUBLESHOOTING GUIDE TO COMPOSTING

Observation	Possible problem	CORRECTIVE ACTION	
		Short-term	Long-term
Pile does not heat up	Not enough nitrogen.	Add nitrogen by mixing in fish, blood meal or manure.	Lab test raw materials for C:N ratio.
	Too wet for aerobic bacteria.	Turn pile and mix in dry carbonaceous material.	Balance pile moisture at 60% average.
	No air penetration.	Turn pile to aerate.	Shred material. Add a granular material. Upgrade turning equipment.
Pile heats slowly.	Low on nitrogen.	Add nitrogen.	
	Not enough air.	Turn pile.	
	Lack proper bacteria.	Add BioActivator.	
Pile overheats and dries out.	Too much aeration.	Pack pile. Add water.	Increase pile density or irrigate pile. Pre-digest manures in low windrows.
Pile smells of ammonia.	Too much nitrogen.	Add carbonaceous material. Mix pile more thoroughly.	Change recipe or turning procedure.
	Too high pH.	Add sulfur.	Use low pH materials.
Pile leaches after rain.	Too moist to absorb additional water.	Turn pile. Use drier materials. Cover pile.	
Anaerobic core in pile.	Uneven pile mix.	Turn pile.	Upgrade turning equipment or procedure.
	Materials that mat.	Turn pile.	Shred materials or switch to granular materials.
Weeds on pile.	Infrequent turning.	Turn pile.	Increase turning frequency. Cover with new material.

If the carbon to nitrogen ratio, moisture content, particle size, and contours of the pile are ideal, there is no further need to manipulate the pile. However if the optimal conditions are not present, then some action may be necessary. If the pile is too wet, an anaerobic core will form, with little temperature increase. The pile must then be turned. If there is not enough moisture, or if microbial heat has driven off the moisture, water must be pumped in or the pile must be packed or spread out.

On a farm scale, the process of reloading the manure spreader and throwing a new parallel pile is much quicker than the first mixing of raw materials. Industrial compost turners mix their piles every few days, as their purpose is to generate a homogenized compost in as little time as possible.

Decisions about whether and when to turn compost can be based on temperature, monitored by long (two- or three-foot) thermometers, or by feel. A composter also develops a fine sense of smell—finished compost has an easily recognized earthy fragrance. Anaerobic cores or the gray mold caused by overheating can be seen when a pile is opened with a spade. Lab analysis of the raw material mix and at various stages of the process may be helpful, but often the senses of the composter can best direct the composting process.

Compost Usage

High-quality finished compost can be spread at any time in any amount, limited mainly by equipment capabilities. The greatest benefit from its inoculating effect is gained by spreading available compost thinly over the total acreage, rather than concentrating on a small area. Differences in raw materials and extent of processing often determine differing uses. Semi-finished compost contains more soluble nutrients, especially nitrogen, and is often used for heavy feeders such as corn. However, the intermediate breakdown products in partially finished compost can be detrimental to germination of some crops. If minerals are needed, they can be blended into the compost at the last turning, or used to create "boosted blends" for special needs like greenhouse media.

Compost fosters the biological processes in the soil. Its use is a major tool in the creation and preservation of soil fertility.

GREEN MANURES AND OTHER SOIL-IMPROVING CROPS

Among the most important ways of building and maintaining soil organic matter is to grow it in place. The obvious benefit of this method is that there is no need to load, haul, and spread large quantities of materials—all you have to do is spread some seed and perhaps add some supplemental nutrients, and the biomass will accumulate as the plants grow, right where it's needed. There are drawbacks, including having to take land out of cash crop production for a period of time and concerns about competition for moisture, but the effort invested in crop planning, and perhaps in some on-farm trials of different green manures, will be amply rewarded in improved tilth and humus content. Recent research indicates that, in areas of low rainfall, subsoil moisture removed by green manure crops is more than offset by improvements gained in the soil's moisture-retention qualities and overall tilth.

Green manures can also be important sources of biological diversity, crucial for ecological pest-control systems. Beyond serving as smother crops, they interrupt pest and disease cycles, and provide a habitat and food source for beneficial insects such as predatory mites, wasps, and spiders. The downside is that crop pests such as tarnished plant bugs may also be harbored in adjoining green manure plantings.

A green manure can be defined as any crop that is tilled in before maturity to improve the soil. It serves mainly as a source of nitrogen (especially legumes) and possibly some organic matter, but may also contribute significant amounts of other essential nutrients. When allowed to reach maturity before incorporation, soil-improving crops may also contribute significantly to soil organic matter. Green manure root systems bring otherwise unavailable nutrients from the subsoil to the surface, and prevent erosion on cultivated land between cropping seasons. The greatest contribution to soil organic matter will be made by those crops that produce the most biomass—usually perennial grass or legume sod crops, which have massive root systems.

Other terms may also be applied to crops grown primarily to benefit the soil, depending on their intended purpose. Terms such as cover crop, smother crop, catch crop, intercrop, and living mulch reflect different ways to use soil-improving crops in farm planning.

Cover crops are used to protect the soil from erosion during the dormant season, and may also help smother weeds, in which case they may be called **smother crops.** They may be undersown or planted after a main crop is harvested, then tilled under at the beginning of the following growing season. Although they usually provide a flush of nutrients as they decompose, cover crops rarely contribute to stable humus formation. Winter rye and oil radish are commonly used fall cover crops in the North, but some farmers prefer crops such as oats or millet, which die over winter and are easy to incorporate in the spring. Southern farmers use drought-tolerant peas and other annual legumes as summer cover crops.

In windswept prairie regions, crops planted to trap snow and improve soil moisture between main crops are called **catch crops**—crop residues or "trash" left on the surface over winter can serve the same end. In humid regions, a catch crop may be planted to prevent nutrients from leaching away.

Rotation plans often include perennial sod crops, grown for two years or more as forage, which become green manure when plowed under in preparation for the next crop. For greater soil benefit, the final cutting of hay may be left in the field. Annuals such as buckwheat and millet are also commonly used as a main-season green manure or smother crop in rotation plans. These and other fast-growing species also serve to protect the soil in preparation for transplants or late-season crops. Annual weeds such as lamb's-quarters and mustard can be used similarly, as long as they are not allowed to form seed.

A green manure planted at the same time as the main crop, between the rows or in alternating strips, is called an **intercrop** or **living mulch**. In temperate regions a low-growing perennial, often clover, can be sown between rows of annual crops. Besides protecting soil that would otherwise be exposed, it adds nitrogen as it grows. Grasses such as annual rye can be mown, and the clippings provide a free mulch to the main crop. Strip cropping of sloping lands, with alternating sod and cultivated crops, is another form of intercropping.

Mulches—living or dead—serve a critical function in tropical soils, reducing soil temperature as well as contributing fresh organic matter. Alley-cropping or agroforestry systems may use perennial legumes, including shrubs and trees, between rows of annual or perennial cash crops. Besides the nitrogen contributed by the legume root systems, the tops may be cut for fodder or as mulch for the main crop, or used to shade crops such as coffee and cocoa. Other types of intercropped plants, such as sunn hemp (*Crotalaria* spp.) can serve as trap crops to attract pest insects away from the main crop.

Selection, Timing, and Management of Green Manures

Just about any plant—including weeds—can be a green manure. The most important considerations are selection of the most appropriate variety for your needs, and timing.

Table 16 lists characteristics of the better-known soil-improving crops. You may be able to get more information about locally adapted species and varieties from Extension or other agricultural agencies. Factors to consider in selecting a green manure include its primary purpose, its adaptability to your soil type and microclimate, its tolerance for adverse conditions, the characteristics

Table 16

GREEN MANURES

Type	When to sow	Seeding rate (lbs. per 1,000 sq. ft.)	Regions where adapted in U.S.	Comments
		LEGUMES		
Alfalfa	Spring	1	all	Deep-rooted, needs good drainage, neutral pH.
Beans, soy	Spring	5	all	Annual.
Beans, fava	Spring or fall	6	all	Annual, edible bean, cold-tolerant.
Clover, alsike	Spring–late summer	0.5	North	Tolerates wet, acid soil.
Clover, crimson	Fall	1	South-Central	Winter annual.
Clover, ladino	Spring–late summer	0.5	all	Tolerates traffic, wet and droughty soil.
Clover, red	Spring–late summer	0.5	North-Central	Perennial, good P-accumulator.
Clover, sweet (yellow or white)	Spring–summer	0.5	all	Needs good drainage and neutral pH. Yellow tolerates dry conditions.
Clover, white Dutch	Spring–summer	0.5	all	Perennial, tolerates traffic.
Cowpeas	Spring	5	South-Central	Drought-resistant annual.
Hairy Indigo	Spring	0.5	Deep South	Needs warm, well-drained soil. Resists root-knot nematod.
Lespedeza	Spring	1	South	Good for restoring eroded, acid soil.
Lupine, white/blue	Spring	1	all	Tender annual, good OM producer.
Pea, field or Austrian	Spring or fall	5	all	Annual, best combined with grain crop field.
Trefoil, birdsfoot	Spring	0.5	all	Comparable to alfalfa but tolerates poor soil.
Vetch, hairy	Spring–fall	1.5	all	Best combined with rye, good biomass producer, winter-hardy.

Type	When to sow	Seeding rate (lbs. per 1,000 sq. ft.)	Regions where adapted in U.S.	Comments
NONLEGUMES				
Barley	Spring or fall	2.5	all	Needs pH 7–8; use spring varieties in North.
Brassicas (kale, radish, etc.)	Spring–fall	0.5	all	Fast-growing, cool-season. Do not allow to set seed.
Bromegrass, smooth	Fall	1	North	Cold-hardy winter cover crop.
Buckwheat	Spring–summer	2–3	all	Tender, good smother crop; P-accumulator.
Millet, pearl	Spring–summer	1	all	Fast-growing warm-season smother crop. Tolerates low pH.
Oats	Spring or fall	2.5	all	Tolerates wide pH range, avoid heavy clay. Good "nurse crop" for legumes.
Rye, winter	Fall	2.5	all	Allelopathic (suppresses weed growth when turned under).
Ryegrass, annual	Spring or fall	1–2	all	Widely adapted, rapid grower.
Sudangrass (and sorghum)	Spring–summer	1	all	Tolerates poor drainage; rapid biomass producer in hot weather.
Wheat, winter	Late summer	2–3	all	Needs pH 7–8, good fertility

TROPICAL GREEN MANURE CROPS, grown under widely varying soil, weather, and seasonal conditions, can include the following: *Aeschynomene, Acacia saman, Azolla, Canavelia, Chromalaena odoratum, Crotalaria, Indigofera, Gliricidia sepium, Mucuna, Pithecellobium dulce, Sesbania rostrata,* and grain legumes such as mung beans.

of your main crop, and, of course, the availability and cost of seed.

Synergistic combinations of different green manures are also possible: a grass and legume are commonly sown together, enhancing the growth of both. Mixtures that include drought-tolerant species with more demanding ones help reduce the strain of poor germination in a dry year. Evaluation of green manures is one area in which on-farm experimentation has become the cutting edge of practical new information on fertility improvement.

Table 17

NITROGEN CONTRIBUTIONS OF GREEN MANURES IN ROTATION

HIGHEST: (OVER 100 POUNDS PER ACRE)

Legumes

- Perennial and biennial (alfalfa, trefoil, red & sweet clover, vetch)
- Turned under as green manure.
- Sod after hay is harvested.*
- Annual (soybeans, field peas) turned under as green manure

MODERATE: (50–100 POUNDS PER ACRE)

- Sod of mixed grass and legume in rotation.*
- Nonlegume annuals turned under as green manure.

LOW: (UNDER 50 POUNDS PER ACRE)

- Sod of perennial grass only.
- Residue after harvest of annual legume crops (soybeans, dry beans, field peas).

*Weight of roots relative to tops increases with age of perennial stand and is highest in early summer of second year for biennials.

Timing is critical, both for sowing and incorporating green manures. Growth cycles must be timed to complement, not compete with, cash crops. Some will grow happily in cold soils, and others can tolerate midsummer conditions. Biennials and perennials produce the most biomass in their second or third year of growth. As the green manure crop grows, its nutrient composition and carbon to nitrogen ratio changes. The trick is to pick the right time to incorporate it, and thereby provide the most benefit to the soil for your effort.

Some characteristics of green manure crops at different stages of growth include:

Early: Young, succulent growth decomposes quickly (with good moisture and aeration), and releases mineralized nutrients for the crops that follow. Carbon to nitrogen ratios are low, so microbes lock up little of the nitrogen, leaving it immediately available to crops. Decomposition is fairly thorough, with little contribution to stable humus.

Midseason: Growth is coarser and may require more powerful cultivating equipment to incorporate. Decomposition is slower, and may not provide surplus nutrients to the crops that follow. Carbon to nitrogen ratios favor maximum microbial growth, and the nutrients they use will become available later in the season. Larger amounts of organic matter are added to the soil, improving structure and tilth.

Late: Beekeepers may wish to use flowering green manures for bee forage. Otherwise, green manures should not be allowed to form seed; if they do, they are no longer considered "green" manures. On poorly drained soils, waiting as long as possible will improve aeration the most; this may be the best time to work the soil. High carbon to nitrogen ratios result in very slow decomposition, with nutrients well protected against leaching.

Whatever its stage of maturity, a green manure is most effective when mixed into the top few inches of soil, rather than being plowed under, where the air supply for microbes is limited. It is best to incorporate green manure in two passes, allowing it to partially dry before final incorporation. This prevents putrefaction caused by excess moisture. Mineral fertilizers and rock powders are often most effective when incorporated with green manures. If spread prior to seeding they will enhance the growth of the green manure, increasing the yield of organic matter. Raw manure can be incorporated with overly mature, carbonaceous green manures, speeding decomposition and humus formation.

ROTATIONS

The only circumstance in which rotations are not necessary in an ecological soil management program is in the case of perennial plantings; even then, a polycultural system using rotated annual intercrops is often valuable. The rotation plan is a key element of your overall farm planning system, which is central to compliance with organic certification requirements.

Whenever cultivated annual crops of any kind are grown, rotation, succession, or intercropping with sod or other perennial crops is necessary, unless large amounts of organic matter are brought in. Rotation of plant types enhances soil fertility by mixing nitrogen-fixing legumes, mineral-accumulating or scavenging plants, and deep-rooting species. Rotations regenerate organic matter exhausted by previous crops by adding crops that maximize biomass or provide sod cover. Rotations also perform the indispensable function of controlling weeds by smothering or allelopathic effects. They also contribute to the control of crop pests without the use of poisons by providing the ecological diversity required by predators and parasites. This biological diversity is matched by a diversity of labor requirements and farm income sources.

Rotation Planning Considerations

Length of Rotation: Analyze conveniently divided portions of fields. Each area suited to the same general crops can be put into the same rotation pattern. If you have as many portions as there are years in your rotation, a good balance of high- and low-income crops can be maintained. In general, longer rotations promote greater ecological complexity, and therefore greater stability. If possible, divide large fields into smaller rotation units.

Soil Characteristics: "Native" organic matter content and fertility, as well as texture, drainage, and slope, will limit which crops are suited to your land. Your options will increase as your ecological management program progresses. Matching crops to soils is an art developed through practice. This is where the experience of neighbors and local agricultural advisors can be most useful. In general, highly fertile, flat land can be cropped most intensively; that is, less of the rotation can be devoted to sod crops and more to crops with high yields and returns. Poor soils may require longer periods in soil-improving crops, until fertility levels can support more intensive production, or may never be suitable for cultivated crops.

Crop Characteristics: The more demanding a crop, the less frequently it should be grown in the same place. Crops that are susceptible to the same soil-borne insects and diseases must be moved around to prevent pest buildups. Forage crops help clean a field of annual weeds, but fine-seeded, slow-germinating crops like carrots have trouble following freshly tilled sod. Alternating deep-rooted and shallow-rooted crops makes subsoil nutrients more available and improves soil structure. Where rainfall is limited, water requirements of succeeding crops must be factored in. Some rotation schemes call for alternating root crops, fruiting crops, and soil-improving crops.

Crops that have particularly heavy demands for one nutrient should be followed by those that need comparatively little of that

Table 18

NUTRIENT DEMANDS OF VARIOUS CROPS

Crop	Nitrogen demands	Phosphorus demands	Potassium demands	Other critical nutrients
FORAGES				
Grass	Mod–High	Moderate	Mod–High	magnesium, iron
Legume	Low	Low–Moderate	High	calcium, molybdenum, boron
Small Grains	Low–Moderate	Low–Moderate	Low–Moderate	magnesium, iron
Corn	High	Low–Moderate	High	zinc, magnesium
Potatoes	High	High	High	manganese
Root Crops	Low	Low–Moderate	Low–Moderate	boron
GARDEN VEGETABLES				
Beans and peas	Low	Moderate	Low–Moderate	calcium, molybdenum, sulfur, zinc
Brassicae (cabbage family)	High	Mod–High	Mod–High	iron, boron, calcium
Cucurbitae (squash, cukes, etc.)	Mod–High	Moderate	Moderate	magnesium
Leaf crops	High	Moderate	Moderate	iron, copper
Onions	Mod–High	Moderate	Low–Moderate	copper, sulfur
Tomatoes (peppers, eggplant)	Moderate	Low–Moderate	Mod–High	iron, magnesium

NOTE: *These guidelines provide general information useful for planning rotations around relative nutrient demands.*

same nutrient, while soil-improving crops should be timed to precede heavy feeders. The common practice of following alfalfa with corn in a rotation can usually provide all the corn's high nitrogen needs. Cultivated row crops should not be grown more than two years in succession and should include a green manure cover between cropping seasons. (Table 18 on page 112 lists nutrient demands of various crops.)

Rotation Effect: Some evidence indicates that certain crops have a beneficial effect on succeeding ones, while other combinations may be detrimental. Brassicas seem to do better following onions, and potatoes following corn, while potatoes seem to be more prone to scab when they follow peas or oats. Cotton following corn has been shown to produce higher yields than either crop alone.

Other Sources of Fertility: As long as any crop or livestock product is sold off the farm, there is little chance of meeting all soil needs through rotations—even when everything else is recycled conscientiously. If your proportion of livestock to cultivated land is high, organic matter levels can be maintained primarily through manure. If you purchase livestock feed, however, you are still buying fertility from off-farm. Other sources of organic matter, such as mulches, may also reduce the need for sod in rotation. Timing of manure, compost, and mineral fertilizer applications should be built into rotation plans, to coincide with crop requirements and optimization of green manures.

Seasonal Labor Needs and Market Availability: Rotations allow you to spread workloads more evenly over the growing season, as long as you plan properly to avoid several crops whose peak labor demands coincide. Specialized equipment may also be needed to plant or harvest certain crops. Crops which work well in a rotation may also be difficult to market, requiring you to factor in a low return per acre or to invest effort in developing new markets. However, the financial risks of crop failure or market fluctuations, which can result from reliance on a single crop, are also diminished.

Sample Rotation Plans

Temperate Zone Vegetables: Mechanized, moderate-scale (Lampkin): Onions–Potatoes–Carrots–Brassicas–Legume forage. This presumes use of manure or compost, and cover crops between seasons (e.g., winter rye after potatoes, and/or buckwheat before carrots).

Small-scale, intensive (Coleman): Legume/green manure–Strawberries (two years)–Carrots–Peas–Brassicas. Also presumes use of manure or compost, and cover crops between carrots–peas and peas–brassicas.

Cash Grain and Livestock: Temperate, moderate moisture: Alfalfa or mixed legume sod (two years)–Corn–Soybeans–Oats or other small grain (serves as nurse crop for forage seeding). An additional year of corn can be included if manure or compost is used. Corn is assumed to be harvested for grain, with stubble left in the field.

Arid Regions: The overriding concern of arid-region farmers when planning a rotation is moisture. They fully understand that the best way to improve the moisture retention of the soil is to add organic matter, but they are reluctant to put a "brown manure" crop in the rotation because of the water it will use in growing. They know from experience that the next cash grain crop will be light unless they receive greater than normal rainfall. The tendency then is to summer-fallow a field after a grain crop. Summer fallowing is simply cultivating a field to keep it bare of moisture-consuming weeds. This practice also lowers soil organic matter and, hence, the health and moisture-retention abilities of the soil. Farmers can only pull out of this vicious downward spiral by developing a rotation that increases soil organic matter content. The real issue is not agronomics but economics; that is, long-term sustainability versus short-term financial survival.

It would be close to impossible to accomplish this change all at once, but it can be done field by field over a period of years. One of the agronomic keys to this transition is cash-crop diversification where some wheat or other grain is replaced by oilseeds such as canola or safflower, and dry fallow periods are used to grow pulse crops that don't use much water. The return of animal stock to prairie farms is another important facet in establishing sound rotations. Legumes such as sweet clover and black medic can also find a place in the rotation, either seeded under grain or sunflower crops, or as strips between grain (left standing they can catch snow in the winter in northern areas). There are numerous moisture-retention tricks that have been developed by organic dryland farmers: the Australian keyline system; the development of chickpea and red lentil crops in Turkey or pea varieties in Saskatchewan; alternate low/high strip-cutting of grain, the planting of windbreaks to reduce evapotranspiration; and stubble mulch tillage practices.

Each farm will have its own optimum rotation, but the basic principles for ecological soil management in dryland areas are:

- minimize the use of summer fallow
- minimize tillage
- maximize biomass incorporation
- add manure and carbon sources when possible
- put as much area under sod as possible

The economic key to this conversion is a shift in government policy from current crop-based commodity programs to increased support for crop-diversification incentives and conservation reserve programs.

Tropical Regions: Tropical crop rotations are determined according to the rainy and dry seasons, which vary widely in intensity, duration, timing, and reliability. The goal is to keep the soil covered continuously, timing plantings to take advantage of moisture for germination and to avoid erosion of exposed soil. Legumes are a desirable component of the rotation scheme due to their soil-building qualities, although many farmers feel they cannot afford to return them to the soil. In some situations two to four crops, including corn, peanuts, yams, millet, beans or other legumes, and a cash crop, are grown together in the same field. This, along with techniques like alley cropping, mulching, and livestock grazing between cropping periods, lessens the need for the classical type of crop rotation.

Permaculture

While rotations may be appropriate for many annual crops in some climatic regions, a permacultural system may be a better ecological design for perennial crops and other climatic regions.

Permaculture is based on the design of cultivated ecosystems modeled on the diversity, stability, and resilience of natural ecosystems. Permaculture utilizes the principles of agroforestry, alley cropping, intercropping, and other polycultural systems. This approach often incorporates a multistory design where tall trees are spaced between short trees and shrubs mixed with annual plants over a ground cover. As with other forms of ecological soil management, permaculture is a synthesis of traditional knowledge and scientific technologies. This information is used in the design process, where plants, animals, and minerals are selected based on site-specific considerations and available managerial and financial resources. The resulting agricultural configuration has built-in feedback loops that can be monitored, evaluated, and modified.

In temperate-zone orchards many permaculture design techniques can be used to increase the ecological diversity thereby enlivening the soil and creating internal, biological pest controls. There is also a set of permacultural practices for arid areas that can slowly increase the moisture retention of the soil/plant system.

Although a permacultural system can be designed for any soil and climatic system, the best examples are currently in the tropics. Organic matter in the soil is continually dissipating in the high-temperature tropics. Thus, tropical soils cleared of their natural forest cover or savanna can quickly lose their productivity. Commercial tropical agriculture has often been implemented with large-scale, temperate-climate-zone methods, specifically monocultural row-cropping with intensive cultivation by high-powered tractors. This style of agriculture is not sustainable in either economic or ecological terms, not to mention its negative social impact. In contrast, many profitable tropical organic farms have developed systems that supply food for local consumption, produce export crops for cash, and improve the soil.

In a Mexican community on the Pacific Coast, sesame is grown as an alley crop between rows of leguminous tamarind trees. Nearby, papaya plants are intercropped in a young mango orchard. Plots of bananas are nestled under coconut trees, while cows and pigs are rotated through various fields. The increasing use of leguminous shrubs, herbs, fruits, and other plants, both traditional and exotic, is taking place on an experimental basis in various hedgerows and shelterbelts. This integrated system protects soil from erosion, increases organic matter content, supplies nitrogen, and has a greater marketable yield at lower cost than row-crop monoculture.

On the thin soils of the mountainous region of Darjeeling in northern India, the traditional tea plantations are faced with massive erosion problems. The causes of this are typical of many regions: trees are being cut for firewood and even the prunings from the tea plants are burned. There is no return of organic matter to the soil or protection for the forest. Landslides are common, and the valleys now flood with every monsoon. Contrast this with the organic tea estate of Makaibari, where two generations of management have created a permaculture model. Tea is the cash crop, and loving care is taken of the plants from the nursery to the field, and through the hand-picked harvest to the diligent fermentation and firing at the estate processing center. There are five villages on the farm and it is among the people there that the system achieves ecological and social legitimacy. Workers on Darjeeling tea estates have firm legal rights to employment and housing. All management programs must receive the tacit endorsement of the workers through their union. The estate workers even have a right to the tea prunings for use as fuel.

In order to implement a permacultural system, management had to make it work for everyone, which is, after all, the real measuring stick of any organic or sustainable system. The transition started with the installation of pilot biogas digestors, which provided methane cooking gas from manure. Cash was provided for the purchase of animals to create the manure supply. Repayment started with the sale of dairy, egg, and meat products. Interest was the leftover sludge from methane production mixed with waste materials in village compost sites. Fodder for the animals was provided on estate land, thus getting the support (or buy-in) for green-manure planting schemes. This planting included leguminous trees, shrubs, and clovers as well as quick-growth plants like Guatemala grass, which was also used to provide mulch (termed "thatch" in tea regions) for the tea plants.

While the Guatemala grass was grown in special areas, the legumes were integrated into the tea plantings. Until recently tea production has had a tradition of using leguminous trees for shade. They also reduce the moisture loss from evapotranspiration, and provide erosion control, nitrogen from fixation, and organic matter from leaf fall. These trees form the top story or canopy layer of a four-story system. The third story consists of leguminous shrub species such as *Glyricidia,* indigo, *Crotalaria,* and *Medolia.* These shrubs can be severely pruned at the beginning of the rainy season to allow air flow and then allowed to releaf in the dry season to provide shade. The prunings are allowed to decompose on the soil surface or provide animal fodder. Neem trees also occupy this story. Their fruit and leaves are harvested to produce an extract sprayed on tea plants to ward off the tea mosquito bug and mites. The extract is also used by everyone as a germicidal wash, toothpaste, and general tonic. Other herbal preparations are used as plant sprays and village medicines in the Indian Ayurvedic tradition.

The tea plants receive a compost mulch at the beginning of the growing season after pruning. At Makaibari the tea prunings are left to decay under the plant in a carpet of low-growing clovers. On the hills and in the valleys the forests are protected from cutting and allowed to grow with only the occasional harvest of leaf litter to provide mulch for nearby new tea plantings. The forest is also home to an incredible variety of insects and animals, which prevents any pest epidemics.

It's a pleasant place for tea workers to live, with the family income supplemented by egg and milk sales to local merchants, a convenient gas cooking range, and happy children who earn their candy money raising, planting, and tending trees and shrubs. Incidentally, the quality of the tea fetched the highest price at the Calcutta auction this past season, while production totals now match previous chemical production figures after a four-year transition period.

USING OFF-FARM NUTRIENT SOURCES

The key to ecological soil management is recycling nutrients via organic matter. On many farms, mineral nutrients must be added to replace those removed by the sale of crops and livestock. Loss of nutrients in other ways—such as leaching, erosion, and fixation in unavailable forms—is minimized when the level of organic matter is high, pH is moderate, and microbial populations are healthy.

When off-farm fertility inputs are needed to supplement nutrients contributed by organic matter management, numerous choices are available. In most cases, materials derived from organic wastes or mined minerals are readily available and desirable. While they may be chosen primarily because they provide particular nutrients observed to be deficient or in high demand by a crop, they generally contain substantial amounts of other major and minor nutrients as well. When you rely on natural materials to replenish nutrients, there is little risk of creating imbalances in the soil ecosystem or of causing pollution by overapplication of soluble nutrients.

Purchasing Natural Fertilizer Materials

Calling a product "organic" has suddenly become a hot selling point. There are probably a hundred companies selling "organic" or "natural" fertilizers, and every day new ones appear. There is

Table 19

COMMON NON-ORGANIC SOURCES OF MINERAL FERTILIZERS

Product	Nutrients supplied & percent analysis	Relative cost	Comments
Lime, calcitic	Calcium: 100% $CaCO_3$	Low	Use as directed by soil test recommendations.
Lime, dolomitic or Hi-Mag	Calcium and magnesium: 90–100% $MgCa(CO_3)_2$	Moderate–low	Best source of magnesium when lime is needed.
Gypsum	Calcium and sulfur: 90–100% $CaSO_4 \cdot 2H_2O$	Low	Used to supply calcium where soil pH is high.
Langbeinite	Sulfur: 22% Potassium: 22% (oxide) Magnesium: 18% (oxide)	Moderate–high	Natural mined rock, soluble without posing danger of salt buildup when used according to soil test recommendations.
Colloidal phosphate	Phosphorus: 22% P_2O_5 Calcium: 27% CaO, trace	Moderate	Analysis varies depending on source.
Rock phosphate	Phosphorus, Calcium, trace	Moderate	Analysis varies depending on source.
Superphosphate	Phosphorus: 20% P_2O_5 Sulfur: 14% Some calcium	Moderate	May be less costly than rock powders per unit phosphorus.
Wood ash	Potassium: 7% Calcium	Low	Overuse can cause excess potassium buildup and salinity.
Granite dust	Potassium: 5% Trace	Low	Very slowly available, but provides long-term reserves. Use mica-rich types only.
Greensand (Glauconite):	Potassium: 5% Trace	Moderate–high	Very low availability.

often ample cause for skepticism. Remember that, although legislation exists for labeling food as "organically produced," there is, as yet, no similar protection for consumers of fertilizer products. Some manufacturers think that adding a little fish or seaweed powder makes an otherwise chemically based fertilizer suddenly "organic." In some cases this is deliberate misrepresentation, but in others it is understandable ignorance.

The more information a manufacturer is willing to provide to you—whether on the label or in response to an inquiry—the more confidence you can have in the integrity of the product. Beware of secret formulas and vaguely described ingredients. Once you know what materials are in the bag, you can make an informed decision about whether you want them in your soil. You may find that cost per pound of nutrients provided is the deciding factor for choosing a particular product from among the many options available.

These products can be valuable because of their convenience and uniformity, when you have special soil needs, and when farm-produced compost isn't available in adequate supply. Beware, though, of any "natural" product that offers a double-digit nutrient analysis; very few natural, high-analysis fertilizer materials contain over 10 percent immediately available nitrogen, phosphorus, or potassium (see table 19, page 120), and this analysis will be diluted if any of these sources is used in a blended product.

If you are involved in or considering applying for organic certification, you should be careful to check with your certifying agency about the permissability of any ingredient before using it on your soil. Many "natural" products contain materials such as Chilean nitrate or soap wastes to boost nitrate or phosphate analysis; these materials may be allowed in some organic certification programs and not in others. Other natural waste products, such as leather meal, may be prohibited altogether. Many commercial fertilizer blends are evaluated and listed by the Organic Materials Review Institute (OMRI), which also publishes a list of generic

---

Fertilizer or Soil Amendment?

What is the difference between fertilizers and soil amendments? These terms are often used interchangeably, but there is a distinction. When you apply a material primarily to provide nutrients to plants, it is considered a fertilizer. This includes high-analysis organic wastes as well as chemicals of synthetic origin.

Soil amendments, while they might contain the same nutrients as fertilizers, are materials used primarily to improve soil tilth. They may contain mostly organic matter, such as compost, or very slow-release minerals, such as greensand. Because their nutrients are not immediately available to plants, or are not considered to be important plant nutrients (e.g., calcium), they may not be sold as fertilizers.

---

materials that are acceptable for organic producers (see the Resources section for contact information). Refer to the box on page 124, "Federal Law and Acceptable Organic Fertilizers," and see chapter 5 for more information about organic certification procedures. If organic certification is not a concern for you, some of these products can be valuable short-term measures to supplement otherwise inadequate soil nutrient levels.

Uncomposted Organic Materials

There is a range of uncomposted organic fertilizers available, generally dried and pulverized waste products of food- or fiber-processing industries. In some cases, livestock feed ingredients such as soybean and alfalfa meal are sold as fertilizers. Many farmers find that using these materials as nitrogen supplements is simpler than putting them through an animal first.

Most of these products are more or less "generic," meaning that dried blood or alfalfa meal packaged by company X is not likely to be different from that sold by company Y. Similarly, mineral fertilizers comprised of finely ground rock powders tend to be comparable from brand to brand, although the quality of some rock mineral deposits is known to vary. Kelp and fish meals may differ depending on species used and how they are processed (for instance, with heat and chemical stabilizers). Refer to table 14, page 98, for information about generic organic wastes.

A major consideration in using industrial organic wastes is the possibility of toxic contamination. Dioxin in paper-mill sludge, cadmium in leather tankage, and high levels of pesticide residues in cotton-gin trash are all of critical concern, in light of the importance of recycling the nutrients in these materials. In some cases, composting the material first will degrade or immobilize the contaminant, but in most cases such materials are not permitted for use in organic production, and many are treated as hazardous wastes under environmental regulations.

Blended products can differ considerably from one another in terms of nutrient content, as well as health and environmental criteria. In such cases it is wise to check out the complete list of ingredients and make sure you feel comfortable about putting all of them in your soil. Then compare the cost; you will generally find that creating your own blend from generic ingredients is much less expensive than paying for the convenience of a specially formulated blended product.

Compost-Based Products

There is an increasing array of compost-based fertilizer products available on the market. While many are aimed primarily at home gardeners, a few cater to the needs of commercial farmers. Locally

FEDERAL LAW AND ACCEPTABLE ORGANIC FERTILIZERS

The use of the word "organic" on a label, according to fertilizer industry guidelines, may simply mean "containing carbon." The term "natural" refers to anything of plant, animal, or mineral origin, regardless of what industrial manipulation it has received in the meantime. The Organic Foods Production Act of 1990 (OFPA) gives some guidelines about which kinds of fertilizer materials are and are not acceptable for organic production, but leaves it to the National Organic Standards Board (NOSB) to make recommendations regarding materials to be included on a list of "allowed synthetic" and "prohibited natural" agricultural inputs. After this list is finalized in regulations it can still be amended through a petition process.

While fertilizers derived from natural sources will be generally permitted, the national standards will place certain restrictions on the use of all farm input materials. To be acceptable for organic farming, any commercial fertilizer product will have to fully disclose all ingredients, so a determination can be made that it contains no prohibited materials.

Before the OFPA was passed, many organic certification programs had started to get away from a strict "natural" versus "synthetic" criterion for evaluating fertilizers. Although there is general agreement that manmade materials have a greater potential for harm, it is also recognized that the "ecological profile" of a material is more important than whether it was dug from the ground or is a by-product of an industrial process. The problems associated with certain natural materials have long been acknowledged. It has taken longer for organic advocates to realize that it's not wise to universally prohibit all synthetics. To cite one instance, elemental sulfur, which is used to control plant diseases and to neutralize soil alkalinity, may be naturally mined or derived from industrial stack scrubbers—and telling the difference is very difficult.

Although the OFPA retained the old distinction of natural versus synthetic, the NOSB and the National Organic Program of the USDA have had to grapple with the question of how to evaluate materials that, though natural, should not be accepted for organic farming, as well as those which should be permitted although they are synthetically derived.

The criteria they are using are the questions most organic farmers would ask of any new material:

- What effects will it have on plant growth and health?
- Is it safe for me to handle?
- Will it affect the safety of the food I grow?
- What will it do to (or for) soil organisms?
- Can it lead to air or water pollution?
- Does its mining, manufacture, or transport harm the environment?
- How energy-intensive is it to make?
- Does it help recycle an existing organic waste product?
- Is there a feasible alternative that may be more environmentally benign?

The most important service rendered by this model is to tell us that answers simply don't exist for many of these questions, even for some of the most commonly used fertilizers. This is because scientists and fertilizer manufacturers have tended to focus their research on one question: Does it increase yields? It is hoped that the process of asking these other questions will lead to increased publicly supported research into fundamental questions of soil biology and ecologically conscious fertility management.

For current information about acceptable organic materials, contact the USDA National Organic Program or your organic certifier of choice (see appendix B).

produced composts are commonly available in bulk, whether made by municipal-yard waste facilities or nearby food processors. Skyrocketing landfill costs in recent years have led many strategically located farmers to set up waste recycling operations to take advantage of free fertilizer materials. In some cases, the tipping fees have ended up generating more income than the farming activities! Refer to page 93 for information about farm-scale composting.

Your choice of a commercial compost-based product will depend on its intended use, as well as knowledge of its ingredients, the composting process used, and the reputation of the manufacturer. There is a wide range of organic waste products being composted, and each presents its own challenges for the industrial composting process.

The main headache for large compost producers is achieving uniformity: it's very difficult to get two batches to come out exactly alike in terms of guaranteed analysis. Some companies have worked this problem out by carefully controlling the compost ingredients and process, but most get around it by amending the finished product with uncomposted organic materials or minerals. If uniformity of texture or nutrient content is not a concern, local bulk composts will certainly be more cost-effective to use.

Composting municipal sludge generally kills diseases that may have been present in the raw sewage, but sludge composts can sometimes contain concentrated amounts of toxic heavy metals: most states forbid the sale of contaminated sludge products as fertilizer. All sewage sludge products are currently prohibited for use in organic production. Mushroom compost, the spent bedding from commercial mushroom production, is another potentially residue-laden material. When in doubt, ask for a laboratory analysis showing a clean bill of health for the product.

Specific Mineral Nutrient Sources

If a farmer needs to correct specific nutrient deficiencies, the most biologically compatible sources of mineral fertilizers are slow-acting rock powders. The advantages of natural rock powders include:

- Less shock to soil organisms than with a heavy dose of soluble compounds.
- Less danger of "burning" plant roots, or of salt buildup in soil.
- Less energy-intensive production methods.
- Unrefined rock deposits contain essential micronutrients.
- Often the cheapest source of the desired nutrient, if total content (including that which is not immediately available) is considered.

Disadvantages of natural rock powders include:

- Large quantities are needed to provide enough available nutrients for immediate crop yields.
- Ineffective in soils that are low in organic matter, and unavailable in alkaline soils.
- Long-range planning is necessary for most effective use.
- Unrefined rock deposits may contain undesirable contaminants.
- Considerable ecological costs of mining and transport.

Some major sources of mineral nutrients are, of course, manure and other organic materials. Average analysis tables can be used for rough estimates of what is provided by these sources (see table 21, page 138). Green manures, including weeds, can also contribute needed minerals by converting "unavailable" soil nutrients into organic matter. When calculating fertilizer needs, the usual procedure is to deduct from total needs (as indicated on soil test results) the amount that will be supplied by available manure. The remainder must then be supplied through other sources.

Soluble mineral fertilizers have a place in ecological soil management, especially in the eastern U.S. and other high-rainfall areas, where some leaching loss is unavoidable. When selecting such materials, choose the alternative least likely to harm soil organisms. Therefore, avoid highly concentrated soluble salts, whether natural or synthetic. When adjusting nutrient levels by applying fertilizers, be aware of *balance*. It is better to uniformly underfertilize than to oversupply one nutrient in relation to the others. Theories about nutrient balances are explained in chapter 2.

Reliance on soil test recommendations is no substitute for a thriving, diverse soil ecosystem. Minerals that promote this goal by satisfying soil organisms should always be chosen in preference to those that provide nutrients needed by plants, but which may inhibit biological activity in the soil. Moreover, as pointed out earlier, most recommendations are only approximations of soil needs. *Building humus is the only way to ensure healthy crops under virtually all circumstances.*

Major Cation Nutrients: Calcium, Magnesium and Potassium

Calcium, a building block of plant tissue, is also essential for the health of microbes. University soil labs rarely test for calcium, but it is generally supplied through lime applications. In most cases it is safe to assume that soil calcium is low if you have a low pH. Lime recommendations are usually determined by a combination of cation exchange capacity (CEC), pH, and, in some cases, aluminum levels. Standard liming recommendations can be followed without hesitation—as long as you watch magnesium levels as well.

Some sources of calcium include calcitic lime, dolomitic lime (also contains magnesium), colloidal phosphate, bone meal, gypsum (where pH is high), and wood ashes (apply in small quantities only). Calcium salts such as chlorides, and hydrated lime or other strong bases, are undesirable as sources of calcium.

Magnesium was largely ignored in conventional fertility recommendations until recently. It behaves similarly to calcium in the soil, and is just as deficient in highly leached, acid soils.

Since magnesium occurs most commonly in combination with calcium or potassium in natural rock deposits (dolomite and langbeinite), it can be difficult to correct a magnesium deficiency if your soil is already well-supplied with calcium and potassium. In that case the best approach may be foliar application of a chelated magnesium source to avoid plant deficiencies. Magnesium sulfate (Epsom salts) is sometimes used, but this is only economical on small areas and must be done with great care.

Some sources of magnesium include dolomitic lime and langbeinite (Sul-Po-Mag and K-Mag are trade names).

Potassium is present in most soils, but is often unavailable to plants. It is also one of the few nutrients that is not an inherent component of organic molecules, though some organic materials contain substantial amounts. Organic matter improves potassium availability mainly by raising the soil's cation exchange capacity (CEC). The only way to store a significant amount of potassium in soil reserves available to plants is on colloidal exchange sites.

Available soil potassium not held by the CEC is quite soluble. Any excess applied as fertilizer will either be lost through leaching or will cause "luxury" consumption by plants: they will keep absorbing it beyond their needs before it is adsorbed onto colloidal exchange sites. This is why some soil labs will recommend "split applications" and side-dressing for potassium.

Large enough quantities of granite dust for use as a potassium source can sometimes be obtained. (Only that which is rich in mica, as opposed to feldspar, is useful as a fertilizer.) Because of its fine particle size, the mineral weathers quickly, releasing about 2 percent of its weight as available potassium during the course of a growing season.

Higher-analysis sources, which are quite soluble, are more feasible for correcting large potassium deficits. The ecological acceptability of a potassium fertilizer depends largely on the other elements in the compound. The most common—and the cheapest— potassium carrier is muriate of potash (potassium chloride). Although it is a natural substance, it is undesirable due to its desiccating and salinizing effects, and residual chloride ions.

Some sources of potassium include Sul-Po-Mag or K-Mag (langbeinite), potassium sulfate (sometimes available in a natural form), wood ash, granite dust, and kelp meal.

Major Anion Nutrients: Nitrogen, Phosphorus, and Sulfur

Although there is such a thing as "anion exchange capacity," it is of little significance for fertility management. Mineralization of organic matter is the major source of anion nutrients, other than soluble forms applied directly to crops.

What follows are guidelines for using supplemental sources of these nutrients when soil organic matter reserves are low. This is only acceptable as a stopgap, short-term strategy: the first priority is always on supplying crop needs through organic matter and humus.

Nitrogen requirements were mentioned earlier under organic matter management. As noted, additional sources of nitrogen may be helpful when mineralization of organic matter cannot match crop needs (such as under cold, wet conditions or during drought), or on transitional soils where humus has not yet reached desired levels.

Higher crop yields may be obtained by using more nitrogen than is naturally provided by organic matter. However, such gains may be produced at the cost of poorer crop quality in terms of percent dry weight, insect resistance, and storage qualities.

There may also be times when crop production is imperiled by nitrogen deficiency, especially on fields with low levels of organic matter. An immediate dose of soluble nitrogen can be provided in several ways. The costs and benefits of each must be considered in light of the situation that confronts you.

Crops can be side-dressed with any available organic material having a heavy nitrogen content (see table 14, page 98), or they can be given a heavy application of manure or compost (twenty tons or more per acre). There are also commercial "organic" formulations that use blood meal, fish emulsion, leather meal, or a similar highly nitrogenous waste product to provide supplemental nitrogen. However, these are usually more costly than manure and may contain harmful contaminants such as heavy metals. Farmers not concerned with organic certification may also consider using certain nonorganic nitrogen sources, such as sodium nitrate (also known as Chilean nitrate). If you are considering entering the organic market, you should refer to the discussion on pages 140–141 before deciding to apply any questionable fertilizer material.

In the long run, the goal of your management program should be to eliminate the need for any such fast-acting "rescue chemistry."

Phosphorus: The problem of maintaining an adequate supply of phosphate is a tricky one. Debates over the best phosphate sources, and how best to ensure its availability, are ongoing in both ecological and conventional circles.

Most soil phosphorus reserves are present in organic matter, so adequate supplies and good mineralization are, as usual, the best insurance for fertility. Organic matter also improves the availability of mineral phosphate sources, whether these are rock powders or artificially concentrated forms. Other factors also influence mineral phosphate availability:

- **Soil Reaction.** Phosphorus from any source quickly becomes insoluble at pH extremes. The optimal pH range for phosphorus availability is between 6.0 and 7.0, but rock phosphate is more available at a pH below 6.0 (see figure 18).

- **Nitrogen.** Increasing available nitrogen improves availability of existing phosphates, up to a point.

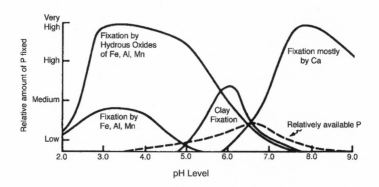

FIGURE 18. *Phosphorus Availability.*

- **Mycorryhizal fungi.** A healthy soil ecosystem promotes the growth of these symbiotic organisms that make phosphorus reserves more available to plant roots.

On soils where phosphate needs are moderate, an application of one ton of hard rock or colloidal phosphate per acre should satisfy crop phosphate requirements for four to five years. Choice of hard rock or black mined phosphate versus colloidal phosphate depends mainly on availability, price, and convenience.

Acid soils are more conducive than alkaline soils to utilization of rock phosphate. For maximum effectiveness, spread rock phosphate uniformly and incorporate it to ensure its availability to soil microbes. The finer the particle size, the more readily available it will be. Rock phosphate is most available when applied:

- With manure, before spreading (also conserving nitrogen), or in compost.
- Before incorporating sod or green manure.
- Prior to seeding legumes in rotation—especially clovers and alfalfa, which are able to make good use of phosphate in this form.

When soil phosphate reserves are low and pH is high, non-organic farmers may want to use artificially concentrated phosphates, such as ordinary super (which is becoming harder to obtain), especially for healthy legume stands. Soluble phosphates do not remain soluble for long, before they are complexed by soil minerals or leached. No matter in what form phosphate is applied, microbial activity is essential for phosphate release and crop growth. Triple superphosphate should be avoided because of its concentrated, acidified nature.

Sulfur is, like nitrogen, an essential part of protein. It can be deficient in soils with depleted humus. Unlike nitrates, sulfates in soluble mineral form pose no threat to soil organisms.

Significant amounts are often found in rainwater, especially in areas that suffer from acid rain. Sulfur deficiencies can also be created when farmers use high-analysis phosphate and nitrate fertilizers (triple super, ammonium nitrate, and urea), instead of lower-grade sources (ordinary super and ammoniated superphosphate) that supply sulfur as well.

If organic matter levels or mineralization rates do not supply enough nitrogen, a supplemental sulfur source may also be needed. A good source of organic nitrogen, however, will generally supply sulfur needs as well. Otherwise, any ecologically compatible sulfur carrier, such as gypsum, can be used, depending on the requirements for any other nutrients it may contain.

In general there is little risk of oversupplying sulfur in relation to nitrogen or carbon, so nutrient sources that also contain sulfur can be applied without fear of burning plants or harming microbial populations. However, because it forms sulfuric acid in the soil solution, sulfur also has the effect of lowering soil pH.

Micronutrient Fertilizers

The behavior and function of micronutrients in soil and plants is complex and not well understood. This alone is a good reason to rely on organic matter and soil biological activity (supplemented with foliar fish and seaweed applications) to supply plants with properly balanced amounts of micronutrients.

However, there may be instances when you have cause to suspect a specific micronutrient deficiency—perhaps plant symptoms, previous crop problems, or soil test results. The safest way to confirm such a suspicion is with plant tissue analysis: most soil tests for micronutrients (boron excepted) are less accurate than plant tissue analysis.

Deficiencies diagnosed in growing crops or orchards are most effectively treated with foliar fertilizers. Deficiencies diagnosed before planting can be corrected by applying specific micronutrient fertilizers, usually available as chelates or frits, to the soil.

Chelates are organic molecules, such as lignin sulfonates, complexed with cation micronutrients to mimic the action of humus. The nutrients are readily available to plants, but don't react with other elements or leach out. **Frits** are micronutrient salts (anion or cation) that have been fused with glass and shattered into a powder. The nutrients are released slowly as the glass dissolves, becoming available to plants at a gradual rate.

Micronutrients must be evenly applied in correct amounts to prevent toxicity. The best time to apply them is while incorporating fresh organic matter, or before seeding a green manure crop. See table 20 for details on some micronutrient fertilizers.

Foliar Fertilization

"Feed the soil, not the plant" is a principle of organic farming, but there are circumstances that warrant direct plant feeding. All plant leaves absorb nutrients such as carbon and sulfur in gaseous form. Leaves are also able, in some situations, to absorb dissolved minerals and translocate them to sites where they are needed in the plant. As we have seen, the use of certain soluble mineral fertilizers may sometimes be warranted as a short-term measure for ensuring healthy crops within a long-term soil-building program.

Table 20
SOLID MICRONUTRIENT FERTILIZERS

Nutrient	Crops with high demand	Sources and analysis	Maximum application
Boron (B)	Apples, brassicae, celery, beets, clover, alfalfa	Borate 65: 20% B Borax: 11.3% B Boron frits: 2–11% B	2.5–5.0 lbs/acre B for high demand crops.
Molybdenum (Mo)	Legumes, cauliflower, lettuce, spinach	Sodium molybdate: 39% Mo Ammonium molybdate: 54% Mo Molybdenumtrioxide: 66% Mo	0.5–1.0 lbs/acre.
Manganese (Mn)	Legumes, small grains, potatoes	Manganous oxide (MnO): 41–68% Manganese sulfate: 26–28% Mn	7–15 lbs/acre Mn. Foliar application often preferred.
Copper (Cu)	Onions, beets, carrots, corn, oats, fruit trees	Copper sulfate: 25.5% Cu, 12.8% S Copper chelates: 9–13% Cu	3–6 lbs/acre Cu in sulfate form. 0.8–2.4 lbs/acre Cu in chelate form.
Zinc (Zn)	Corn, fruit and nut trees, legumes	Zinc sulfate: 35% Zn Zinc oxide: 78% Zn Zinc chelates: 9–14% Zn	20–40 lbs/acre Zn.

Foliar fertilizers may be used as a stopgap remedy for definite nutrient deficiencies until the soil is able to supply them. Foliar supplementation may also be necessary as an annual practice in some soil and climate situations. In cold northern soils, foliar fertilizers may be necessary each spring to supply nitrogen and phosphorus. In alkaline and high organic matter (peat and muck) soils, micronutrient sprays like iron may be necessary, since certain soil minerals may never be available under these conditions.

FIGURE 19. *Cross-Section of a Leaf. Foliar applied nutrients are absorbed through the epidermis and stoma and translocated through the vascular system.* (Drawing by Stewart Hoyt.)

Liquid seaweed extract and fish emulsion are popular among ecological farmers and gardeners. The seaweed or kelp plant itself illustrates the principle of foliar feeding. It is anchored to the seabed by holdfasts, not roots, and feeds through its leaves from mineral-rich ocean water. Since it balances these mineral inputs and binds them into organic molecular structures (in the process known as **chelation**), the cell sap extract becomes a very useful foliar fertilizer.

There are many factors to consider when you manipulate plant growth through foliar fertilization. Some minerals (such as calcium and boron) are easily absorbed but poorly translocated, while others (such as iron and copper) move easily through the vascular system but don't readily cross the leaf epidermis (see figure 19). Temperature, light, oxygen, pH, and energy availability all affect leaf absorption, but the most important factor is leaf surface moisture.

The best time for foliar fertilization is in the early morning of a cloudy, humid day. Effectiveness increases with the fineness of the spray droplets. A small amount of surfactant added to the mix will de-ionize the leaf surface, improving absorption of the material. Timing of sprays should also coincide with the stage of plant growth when nutrients are in high demand by the plant but root intake is low.

Leaves can only accept small amounts of mineral materials. Therefore micronutrients lend themselves to foliar application, but significant amounts of major nutrients cannot be supplied in this way. When some elements (such as calcium, magnesium, iron, manganese, molybdenum, and copper) are chelated, they are more easily absorbed than as a mineral salt. There is a controversy in organic circles about "synthetic" chelates, and some research indicates that these chelates may tie up plant minerals after delivering their nutrient. The most acceptable synthetic chelating agent for ecological farmers is lignin sulfonate. Natural chelates, like liquid seaweed extract or mineral salts chelated by processing with molasses, are generally accepted.

Another controversial aspect of foliar spraying is the use of growth-promoting substances. Liquid seaweed has been touted for years by ecological agriculturists as a general-purpose trace mineral

Table 21

FOLIAR FERTILIZATION

Product & Analysis	When to use	Comments
FISH EMULSION		
4-4-1 (N-P-K) varies by manufacturer.	Transplanting, and any time crops need an extra N and P boost, as in early spring: Dilute 20:1.	As a general rule, one gallon will treat one acre of crops at a time (2–4 gal/season).
LIQUID SEAWEED CONCENTRATE		
Contains more than 1% of K, Ca, Na, Cl, S, and about 50 other minerals in trace amounts. Also plant hormones such as auxins and cytokinins.	Transplanting and rooting cuttings: Dilute 25:1. Flower bud and petal fall (fruit crops): Dilute 40:1. To alleviate stress (from drought, cold, etc.) and promote strong regrowth of hay: Dilute 40:1.	Use at most 1.5 gallons per acre per season. If blending fish and seaweed together, dilute one before adding the other. It is sometimes helpful to use a surfactant (wetting agent) to aid even spray distribution. Best time to spray any foliar nutrient is early morning or evening, never in full sun.
SOLUBLE MICRONUTRIENTS		
All sulfates and chelates of Mn, Fe, Cu, and Zn can be used in foliar applications, as well as Mo salts. B is available as Solubor™ (20.5% B) or boric acid (17.5% B).	All should be used only when indicated by plant tissue analysis, or when a soil deficiency is known to exist. In general, a lower rate of application (in lbs/acre) is needed to correct deficiencies than when soil applied.	B is rarely recommended for foliar application, except on apples. Mo solutions can be used to soak legume seeds when inoculating. Always explore the possibility that deficiencies are due to soil imbalances.

spray and growth promoter. It contains several hormones, including auxins, gibberellins and cytokinins. All of these are chemical messengers produced naturally in minute quantities by the plant. Cytokinins are of particular importance, since they increase the speed of cell division. Introducing hormones from elsewhere increases growth rates or breaks dormancy earlier than the plant ordinarily would do so.

5

THE MARKETPLACE AND ORGANIC CERTIFICATION

In the past ten years the market for organically produced goods has exploded, and is estimated to be growing by more than 20 percent each year. This burgeoning market demand for certified organic foods, often accompanied by substantial price premiums, has been a primary incentive for farmers to explore more ecological management systems. In producing for this market, certain standards must be met. These can vary somewhat according to the certifying organization, but in many countries these standards are now subject to government regulation. In the international arena, the Codex Alimentarius Commission of the United Nations has been preparing guidelines since 1990 that may set the protocol for international trade in organic food. In the U.S., the passage of the Organic Foods Production Act (OFPA) in the 1990 farm bill set the rules, with detailed regulations still to be enacted. Once the final regulations are implemented, all products labeled "organic" will have to be certified according to federal requirements. Organic products imported into the U.S. will have to be certified under a program that is considered to be equivalent to that of the U.S.

While many provisions of this legislation are controversial, it has for the first time established an expectation of a unified set of national standards that precisely define organic production methods. It is also significant in placing heavy emphasis on soil quality and a sound soil management plan as criteria for evaluating applicants for certification. The final regulations will include stipulations about which specific materials (including many kinds of farm inputs, such as pest controls and livestock feed, in addition to fertilizers) are acceptable for use in organic production.

If you are planning to sell to the organic market, there should be little difficulty in using any of the methods outlined in this book. It is essential, however, that you contact the certification program you intend to work with (information about how to find them is given in appendix B) concerning specific requirements and regulations before you use any material you are unsure about. While all will have to comply with OFPA, until the law is implemented there will remain some variation in standards and other requirements, such as testing regimes, established by independent certification programs. All such programs currently require a transition period of three years after use of any prohibited material (including fertilizers) until a given field can be approved for organic certification.

Whatever the requirements of your certifying organization, proper recordkeeping and a farm plan are musts (refer to pages 53–55). It must be possible to trace, on paper, which fertilizers and pest control materials were purchased, where and when they were applied, and at what rates. In addition, you should have some system for keying sold crops to their field of origin by lot number. Inventories of materials on hand that fall into regulated or prohibited categories must be scrupulously recorded, especially if some portion of your farm is not under organic certification, and there must be no chance of intermingling products that are organic with those that are not. Taking great care with paperwork or computerized recordkeeping avoids possible doubt or misunderstanding, and creates a valuable resource for your own planning and management.

Even federal legislation and its regulatory interpretation is not written in stone. The rules should change as better information becomes available. It is, however, important to develop and maintain marketplace credibility for organic foods, and therefore unwise to risk confusing consumers with contradictory definitions. The process of marketplace education goes hand in hand with the education of producers, who must balance their need for ecologically sound, profitable management tools with their responsibility to uphold consumer trust in their products.

The best guarantee for any consumer is still a face-to-face, personal relationship with the farmer. The rising popularity of direct marketing of all kinds, such as farmers' markets, attests to increased awareness of this fact among consumers. Community supported agriculture, an enterprise in which consumers buy shares of a farm's production on a seasonal basis, has also been expanding rapidly throughout the U.S., in part because it allows consumers to feel more involved in the source of their food. Forming alliances with consumer organizations that make the connection between environmental protection and ecological agriculture is also an important strategy for the farm community. In the future, forms of eco-labeling other than organic will likely gain in marketability. Such "clean and green" labels will also demand adherence to standards and some kind of certification procedure.

Participation in organic certification programs will increase your planning, marketing, and communication skills. The organic marketplace offers an opportunity for ecological farmers to improve their profitability. Widespread adoption of ecological agriculture can only be assured by making it economically viable.

Appendix A

GLOSSARY

Absorption: The taking up of elements or compounds in solution as part of the stream of solvent (such as plant nutrients in water).

Adsorption: Attraction of charged particles to a solid surface of the opposite charge, as in the attachment of cations to soil colloids.

Aerobic: A process that requires the presence of free oxygen, or a condition in which free oxygen is present.

Aggregate: A collection of soil particles that holds together, forming the basis for good soil structure.

Alfisol: Moist mineral soils with high base status and presence of silicate clays, found mostly in humid regions under deciduous forest or grass.

Allelopathy: Suppression of one plant species by another through secretion of phytotoxic exudates.

Anaerobic: A process that does not require free oxygen, or a condition in which free oxygen is excluded.

Anion: A negatively charged chemical element or radical that is acid-forming.

Aridisols: Soils common to deserts; can be productive if irrigated, but care must be taken to avoid the accumulation of soluble salts (see salinization).

Autotroph: An organism, usually a green plant, that uses inorganic materials to synthesize its own food through the process of photosynthesis.

Base saturation: The proportion of total cation exchange sites in a given soil occupied by bases (cations other than hydrogen or aluminum).

Biodynamics: A school of agricultural thought, based on the spiritual teachings of Rudolph Steiner, that views the living interrelationships of soil, farm, and community as an organic whole.

Biomass: The total weight of vegetation growing on a given area of soil.

Bioregion: A geographic area defined by common ecological characteristics, such as climate, soil types, topography, predominant vegetation, and water system.

Brix scale: A measure of percent of sugar content of a liquid, usually cell sap or fruit juice.

Bulk density: One of three measures used to evaluate soil compaction. Represents the weight of a given volume of soil.

Calibrate: To establish the relationship between laboratory soil test values and yield response from incremental rates of the nutrient applied in the field.

Capillary action: The ability of soil to wick up moisture from deeper levels as it is needed, made possible by good structure.

Carbon to nitrogen ratio: The proportion of carbon to nitrogen by weight in any organic matter. The optimum level for biological activity in raw organic matter is between 20:1 and 30:1.

Catch crops: In prairie regions, crops planted to trap moisture between crops.

Cation: A positively charged chemical element or radical, usually alkaline-forming.

Cation exchange capacity (CEC): The capacity of the colloidal particles in a given soil to hold positively charged ions (cations).

Chelate: A compound consisting of a metallic element bound within a complex organic molecule, or the process of forming such a compound (chelation).

Climax ecosystem: The plant/animal/soil community that is most stable and well-adapted to a particular geographic locale.

Colloid: A mass of very fine particles having a high ratio of surface area to weight, and characterized by a gooey consistency. Examples include protoplasm, clay, humus, and mayonnaise.

Compost: A process that uses any one of several methods to speed up the decomposition of raw organic matter, usually by piling, aerating, and moistening. Also, the crumbly, nutrient-rich product of this process.

Consumers: Organisms that obtain nourishment by consuming the products or remains of other living organisms.

Correlate: To express the relationship between amounts of nutrient extracted by laboratory tests and uptake by plants in the greenhouse or field.

Cover crop: A crop used to protect soil from erosion, at the same time building organic matter and controlling weeds.

Decomposers: Organisms, usually soil bacteria, that derive nourishment by breaking down the remains or wastes of other living organisms into simple organic compounds.

Ecology: The science that studies the interrelationships between living organisms and their environment.

Entisols: Recently formed mineral soils. May be highly productive, but most are relatively barren.

Exudates: Biochemical compounds secreted by plant roots.

Fertilizer: Any material added to the soil for the purpose of providing essential nutrients to plants.

Fixation: The binding of a nutrient into a more stable form that may either be less available to plants (as when phosphorus is fixed by calcium and aluminum), or more available to plants (as when atmospheric nitrogen is biologically fixed by bacteria).

Frits: Micronutrient salts that have been fused with glass and shattered into a powder. Used as fertilizer, the nutrients are released slowly as the glass dissolves, becoming available to plants at a gradual rate.

Green manure: A crop that is incorporated into the soil before reaching full maturity, for the purpose of soil improvement.

Hardpan: A heavily compacted subsoil layer, sometimes naturally occurring, but usually created by poor soil management practices.

Heterotroph: An organism whose nourishment depends on organic materials produced by other living organisms.

Histosol: Soils developed in a water-saturated environment, with at least twenty percent organic content. Can be productive if drained.

Horizon: A distinct layer of soil (parallel to the surface) that characterizes the soil-forming process in a particular locale.

Humus: The fragrant, spongy, nutrient-rich material resulting from decomposition of organic matter.

Immobilization: The conversion of an element to a form that is not available for biological processes or chemical reactions. Soil nutrients may be immobilized in microbial or plant tissues, or in very stable chemical complexes.

Inceptisol: Young soils with limited horizon formation. May be very productive, as those formed from volcanic ash.

Inoculant: The spores of the desired strain of rhizobia bacteria, applied in powder form to the appropriate legume seed when planted. Also, any material of high microbial content added to soil or compost to stimulate biological activity.

Intercrop: See Living mulch.

Leaching: The downward movement through soil of chemical substances dissolved in water.

Legume: A member of the plant family that includes clover, alfalfa, beans, and peas, whose roots host nitrogen-fixing rhizobia bacteria in a symbiotic relationship.

Living mulch: A green manure planted at the same time as the main crop. Can protect soil from erosion and add nitrogen to soil, a well as providing mulch.

Macronutrient: A plant nutrient needed in substantial quantities, including carbon, nitrogen, phosphorus, sulfur, calcium, magnesium and potassium.

Metabolism: The sum of the biochemical processes of growth, maintenance, and energy transformation carried out by a living organism.

Micronutrient: A plant nutrient needed in very small quantities, including copper, zinc, iron, manganese, boron, and molybdenum.

Mineralization: The release of soluble minerals and simple organic compounds through the decomposition of organic matter.

Mollisols: Among the most naturally productive soils, with high native organic matter and mineral content. Common on prairies.

Mucigel: A gelatinous material surrounding the root of a plant, created by the root-soil-microbe complex.

Mycorrhizal association: A symbiotic relationship between mycorrhizal fungi and plant roots, in which soil phosphorus is made more available to plants.

Nitrogen cycle: The process by which nitrogen passes from a gaseous state, through living tissue in various organisms, and back into the atmosphere. Carbon and sulfur undergo similar cycles.

Organic matter: The remains, residues, or waste products of any living organism.

Oxisol: The most highly weathered soils, with deep subsurface horizon of iron and aluminum oxides. High in clay, deficient in phosphates and micronutrients.

Oxygen diffusion rate. One of three measures used to evaluate soil compaction. Measures how readily air passes through soil.

Parent material: The raw material—native rock or organic matter—from which topsoil is created through biogeochemical processes and weathering.

Pathogen: An organism capable of causing disease in other organisms.

Permaculture: A term invented by Bill Mollison, who defines it as "the conscious design and maintenanc eof agriculturativ productiv ecosystems that have the diversity, stability, and resilience of natural ecosystems."

pH: The concentration of hydrogen ions in a solution that determines its level of acidity or alkalinity. A pH of 7.0 is neutral; lower numbers indicate acid, and higher numbers indicate alkaline conditions.

Phytotoxin: A substance toxic to plants.

Plowpan: A heavily compacted subsoil layer created by overuse of a moldboard plow.

Profile: The pattern of soil horizons, from topsoil to subsoil, that identifies a particular soil type.

Pore space: The space between soil particles where air and water circulate.

Producers: Organisms, generally green plants, that can make their own food from inorganic materials, usually through the use of radiant energy in photosynthesis.

Putrefaction: The process of anaerobic decomposition, so-called because it often produces foul odors.

Raw manure: Manure that has not yet decomposed, containing highly soluble nitrogen and potassium.

Refractometer: A hand-held instrument that measures the sugar content of any liquid.

Rhizobia: Nitrogen-fixing bacteria that live in symbiosis with legumes.

Rhizosphere: The area immediately surrounding plant roots, where the highest level of soil biological activity exists.

Salinization: The build-up of salts on the surface layer of soil. Often caused by improper irrigation of naturally alkaline soils.

Sheet composting: A method of composting in which organic wastes are incorporated directly into the soil.

Smother crops: Cover crops used to smother weeds.

Soil amendment: Any material added to the soil in order to enhance soil biological activity.

Spodosols: Soils formed from coarse-textured parent material, usually acidic and low in mineral nutrients. Found in temperate, forested regions.

Structure: The physical arrangement—shape, size, and stability—of soil particles.

Symbiosis: A mutually beneficial relationship between two living organisms, such as plant roots and rhizobia.

Synergy: The mutual enhancement of two or more factors (such as soil nutrients), which exceeds the expected sum of individual effects.

Texture: The proportions of sand, silt, and clay in a particular soil.

Tilth: The physical quality or condition of soil, similar to the health of a living organism.

Ultisols: Heavily leached tropical soils that tend to be acidic.

Valence: The electrical charge of a chemical ion, indicating the number of electrons it will accept (for anions) or give up (for cations) in a chemical reaction.

Vertisol: Mineral soils with a high content of selling-type clays, which in dry seasons cause soils to crack. Difficult to cultivate.

Volatilization: The escape of chemical elements into the atmosphere after being transformed into a gaseous state.

Appendix B

ORGANIZATIONS
AND PERIODICALS

The number of organizations and publications serving ecological agriculture is proliferating rapidly. A few key contact groups are listed here, but more extensive and local listings may be found in the following directories, or by contacting one of the national organizations.

Directories

The Organic Pages: Organic Trade Association's
North American Resource Directory
Organic Trade Association
P.O. Box 1078
Greenfield, MA 01301
(413) 774-7511; fax (408) 426-6670

A well-indexed listing of all OTA members, organized by type of enterprise.
Published annually.

National Organic Directory: A Guide to Organic Information
& Resources
Community Alliance with Family Farmers
P.O. Box 464
Davis, CA 95617
(916) 756-8518; FAX (916) 756-7857

Catalogue of Healthy Food
Edited by John Tepper Marlin with Domenick M. Bertelli
Bantam Publishing, 1990

Organizations, Publications, and Web Sites

Acres U.S.A.: A Voice for Eco-Agriculture
Box 9547
Raytown, MO 64133
info@acresusa.com; www.acresusa.com
Monthly publication, with books and annual conference.

Alternative Farming Systems Information Center
National Agriculture Library, Room 111
10301 Baltimore Boulevard
Beltsville, MD 20705
Phone: (301) 344-3704
afsic@nal.usda.gov; www.nal.usda.gov/afsic
Bibliographies and literature searches on all aspects of alternative agriculture.

Appropriate Technology Transfer for Rural Areas (ATTRA)
P.O. Box 3657
Fayetteville, AR 72702
(800) 346-9140
(501) 442-9824; FAX (501) 442-9842
askattra@ncatark.uark.edu; www.attra.org
Information service funded through the National Center for Appropriate Technology (NCAT). Information packets on many aspects of sustainable agriculture. Web site includes helpful listings of alternative soil-testing laboratories and sources of organic fertilizers and amendments.

Bio-Dynamic Farming & Gardening Association
P.O. Box 550
Kimberton, PA 19442
(215) 935-7797; fax (215) 983-3196
www.biodynamics.com
Membership organization with chapters throughout North America, quarterly publication, books, films.

Biological Agriculture and Horticulture
P.O. Box 97
Berkhamsted, Herts HP4 2PX, England
Academic journal featuring the most advanced European work.

Ecological Agriculture Project
Box 225
Macdonald College
Ste. Anne-de-Bellevue, Quebec H9X 1CO, Canada
(514) 398-7771; fax (514) 398-7990
info@eap.mcgill.ca; www.eap.mcgill.ca
Bibliographies, article files, publications, audiovisuals.

International Federation of Organic Agriculture Movements (IFOAM)
General Secretariat
c/o Okozentrum Insbach
D-66636 Tholey, Germany
Phone: 49 (0) 6853-5190; fax 49 (0) 6853-3011
ifoam@t-online.de; http://ecoweb.dk/ifoam
Membership organization with conferences, newsletter and publications.

Journal of Soil & Water Conservation
7515 N.E. Ankeny Road
Ankeny, IA 50021
(515) 289-2331; fax (515) 289-1227

Organic Farming Research Foundation
P.O. Box 440
Santa Cruz, CA 95061
(408) 426-6606; fax (408) 426-6670
research@ofrf.org; www.ofrf.org

Nonprofit foundation dedicated to fostering the improvement and widespread adoption of organic farming practices. Contact them for grant guidelines and applications.

Organic Materials Review Institute
Box 11558
Eugene, OR 97440-3758
(541) 343-7600; fax (541) 343-8971

The mission of OMRI is to publish and disseminate generic and specific (brand name) lists of materials allowed and prohibited for use in the production, processing, and handling of organic food and fiber. They also conduct scientific research and education on the use of materials by the organic industry.

Organic Trade Association
P.O. Box 1078
Greenfield, MA 01301
(413) 774-7511; fax (413) 774-6432
ota@igc.apc.org; www.ota.com

Trade association for the organic food industry, offering political action, consumer information, newsletter, and support for organic marketing.

Rodale Institute
22 Main Street
Emmaus, PA 18098
(610) 967-8108; fax (610) 967-8959
www.envirolink.org/seel/rodale

Nonprofit educational arm of Rodale Press.

Sustainable Farming Connection
http://metalab.unc.edu/farming-connection

Click on Links and Soil Health, or check out the Soil Health menu from the home page. This will take you anywhere in the world of alternative agriculture you want to go.

Wallace Institute for Alternative Agriculture
900 Edmonston Road, Suite 117
Greenbelt, MD 20770
(301) 441-8777
hawiaa@access.digex.net; www.hawiaa.org

National membership organization with newsletter, conferences, and scientific journal for alternative agriculture.

Woods End Research Laboratory
Box 4050
Old Rome, Mount Vernon, ME 04352
(207) 293-2457
info@woodsend.org; www.biomaine.org/woods.html
Research, publications, soil testing, and consultation. Specialists in compost systems and evaluation, including a new test kit for compost maturity.

Organic Certifiers

For a complete listing of private and state organic certification organizations and the status of implementation of the National Organic Program, contact:

National Organic Program
USDA/AMS/TMD
Room 2510-South, P.O.Box 96456
Washington, D.C. 20090
(202) 720-3252; fax (202) 205-7808
www.ams.usda.gov/nop

Organic Farm Organizations

The following regional organic farm organizations offer publications, conferences, workshops, and other education, in addition to organic certification services. Consult one of the directories at the beginning of this section for a complete listing.

Carolina Farm Stewardship Association
115 West Main Street
Carrboro, NC 27510
(919) 968-1030

Community Alliance with Family Farmers (CAFF)
P.O. Box 464
Davis, CA 95617
(916) 756-8518; fax (916) 765-7857

Northeast Organic Farming Association (NOFA)
411 Sheldon Road
Barre, MA 01005
(978) 355-2853
Chapters in CT, NH, NJ, NY, RI, VT.

Northern Plains Sustainable Agriculture Society
Box 36
Maida, ND 58255
(701) 256-2424

Ohio Ecological Food & Farming Association
65 Plymouth Street
Plymouth, OH 44865
(419) 687-7665

BIBLIOGRAPHY

GENERAL REFERENCES

We recommend books in this list for the general lay reader interested in learning more about the practice of ecological agriculture.

Albrecht, W.A. *The Albrecht Papers I & II*. Raytown, Mo: Acres USA, 1975. These books are collections of Albrecht's viewpoints on soil chemistry, soil fertility, and plant, animal, and human nutrition.

Altieri, Miguel A, et al. *Agroecology: The Science of Sustainable Agriculture*. 2nd ed. Boulder, Colo.: Westview Press, 1995.

Ardapple-Kindberg, Eric and Beth. *Soil Fertility for Organic Farmers*. Bass, Ariz: Keyline Environmental Management Systems, 1991. A short guide to practical farming.

Balfour, Eve. *The Living Soil and the Haughley Experiment*. London: Faber & Faber, 1975. This edition of the 1948 classic summarizes the 32-year organic versus chemical trials at Haughley.

Berry, Wendell. *The Unsettling of America: Culture and Agriculture*. San Francisco: Sierra Club Books, 1977. This Kentucky farmer/poet has been a major spokesperson for a sane approach to agriculture. His poetic eloquence is grounded in practical knowledge.

Coleman, Eliot. *The New Organic Grower: A Master's Manual of Tools and Techniques for the Home and Market Gardener*. Revised edition. White River Jct., Vt.: Chelsea Green, 1995. Good basic manual drawn from Coleman's 25 years of experience.

Darwin, Charles. *The Formation of Vegetable Mould through Action of Worms, with Observations on Their Habits*. New York: John Wiley & Sons, 1978. This book, which Darwin thought to be his most important work, is still an unsurpassed account of the earthworm's role in the creation of soil fertility.

Faulkner, Edward. *Plowman's Folly*. Norman, Okla.: University of Oklahoma Press, 1943. An impassioned plea to end the widespread use of the moldboard plow.

Fryer, Lee. *The New Organic Manifesto*. Wheaton, Md.: Earth Foods Associates, 1986.

———. *Food Power from the Sea*. New York: Mason & Charter, 1977. Lee Fryer, a veteran of the fertilizer industry, provides an approach for organic growing and marketing.

Fukuoka, Masanobu. *The Natural Way of Farming*. New York: Japan Publications, 1987.

———. *The One Straw Revolution*. Emmaus, Pa.: Rodale Press, 1978. Fukuoka's techniques mimic nature in the design and management of farming systems.

Gershuny, Grace. *Start with the Soil*. Emmaus, Pa.: Rodale Press, 1993. Straightforward guide to organic soil improvement.

Gliessman, Stephen R., ed. *Agroecology: Researching the Ecological Basis for Sustainable Agriculture*. New York: Springer-Verlag, 1989.

Granatstein, David. *Amber Waves*. Pullman, Wash.: Washington State University, 1992. A sourcebook for sustainable dryland farming.

Howard, Albert. *An Agricultural Testament*. London: Oxford University Press, 1940.

———. *Soil and Health*. New York: Schocken Books, 1947. Sir Albert Howard developed the Indore composting system for tropical climates, and articulated the ecological viewpoint on the value and formation of humus.

Hyams, Edward. *Soil and Civilization*. London: Thames & Hudson, 1952. "Those who do not learn from history are condemned to repeat it."

King, F.H. *Farmers of Forty Centuries*. Emmaus, Pa: Rodale Press, facsimile of 1911 edition. King was the head of Soil Management at USDA, and reports, somewhat romantically, on the careful attention paid to ecological cycles by the Chinese peasant farmer.

Koepf, H.H., B.D. Petterson, and W. Schaumann. *Bio-Dynamic Agriculture*. Spring Valley, N.Y.: Anthroposophic Press, 1976. This is the most practical introduction to the biodynamic method available. The nature and history of the biodynamic movement are explained, showing how the metaphysical source of its theory is not at odds with solid farm practice.

Lampkin, Nicolas. *Organic Farming*. Ipswich, UK: Farming Press, 1990. A comprehensive British scientific textbook on organic practice, not theory.

Magdoff, Fred. *Building Soils for Better Crops: Organic Matter Management*. Lincoln, Nebr.: University of Nebraska Press, 1992. Clearly written, authoritative book giving research findings on the nature, role, and function of soil organic matter—how it is built and how it is lost.

Martin, Deborah, and Grace Gershuny. *The Rodale Book of Composting.* Emmaus, Pa.: Rodale Press, 1992. A gardener's guide to the principles and practices of composting.

Mollison, Bill. *Permaculture: A Designer's Manual.* Tyalgum, NSW, Australia: Tagari Publications, 1992.

———, with Reny Slay. *Introduction to Permaculture.* Tyalgum, NSW, Australia: Tagari Publications, 1991. The bible of sustainable agricultural design strategies.

Parnes, Robert. *Fertile Soil: A Grower's Guide to Organic & Inorganic Fertilizers.* Davis, Calif.: agAccess, 1990. An excellent guide to fertilization practice, with a somewhat radical emphasis on carbon.

Pfeiffer, Ehrenfried E. *Bio-Dynamic Farming and Gardening,* vols. 1–3. Spring Valley, N.Y.: Anthroposophic Press, 1983.

———. *Chromatography Applied to Quality Testing.* Wyoming, R.I.: Bio-Dynamic Literature, 1959.

———. *Compost Manufacturer's Manual.* Spring Valley, N.Y.: Anthroposophic Press, 1950.

———. *Soil Fertility: Renewal and Preservation.* Spring Valley, N.Y.: Anthroposophic Press, 1943.

———. *Weeds and What They Tell.* Wyoming, R.I.: Bio-Dynamic Literature, 1981. Dr. Ehrenfried Pfeiffer, a student of Rudolf Steiner, was a seminal influence on ecological agriculture in North America. His scientific rigor established a standard of excellence for ecological practitioners to follow.

Rateaver, Bargyla. *The Organic Method Primer.* San Diego: Rateavers Press, 1993. A new edition of one of the best books on organic gardening, with a new section on plant absorption of nutrients that refutes the concept of ion exchange.

Reijntjes, Haverkort, and Waters-Bayer. *Farming for the Future.* London: Macmillan, 1992. An excellent introduction to low external input and sustainable agriculture for the tropics, with an invaluable annotated reference section.

Rodale Press Staff. *Controlling Weeds with Fewer Chemicals, Profitable Farming Now!* and *The Farmer's Fertilizer Handbook.* Emmaus, Pa.: Rodale Press, various dates. These books are collections of articles from *The New Farm* magazine and special reports. They offer a hands-on, practical approach to regenerative agriculture.

Sarrantonio, Marianne. *Methodologies for Screening Soil-Improving Legumes.* Rodale Institute, 1991. A unique, practical guide to choosing the best legumes for cover crops or green manures.

Savory, Allen. *Holistic Resource Management.* Washington, D.C.: Island Press, 1988. A systems approach to managing resource systems. This method has been most widely implemented with intensive grazing.

Schriefer, D. *From the Soil Up.* Des Moines, Iowa: Wallace-Homestead, 1984. The best book available on the principles and practice of tillage.

Smith, Miranda, et al. *The Real Dirt.* Burlington, Vt.: Sustainable Ag Publications, 1994. First-hand knowledge from more than 60 Northeast farmers on the many biological, cultural, mechanical, and even chemical tools available for reduced-input farming.

Steiner, Rudolf. *Agriculture.* Spring Valley, N.Y.: Anthroposophic Press, 1928. This is the record of eight lectures on agriculture given by Rudolf Steiner in 1924. He describes in metaphysical terms the interplay of terrestrial and cosmic forces that create the processes of agriculture.

Storl, W.D. *Culture and Horticulture: A Philosophy of Gardening.* Wyoming, R.I.: Bio-Dynamic Literature, 1979. One of the most readable and easy-to-comprehend explanations of biodynamic theory.

Sykes, F. *Humus and the Farmer.* London: Faber & Faber, 1949.

———. *Modern Humus Farming.* London: Faber & Faber, 1959. These are practical books on biological soil management, written by an experienced and articulate British farmer.

Tompkins, Peter, and Christopher Bird. *Secrets of the Soil.* New York: Harper & Row, 1989. Strongly informed by biodynamics, this book is an overview of the various fringe practitioners of agricultural science, from Hieronymus to Perelandra.

Turner, N. *Fertility Pastures and Cover Crops.* London: Faber & Faber, 1955. This British farmer concentrates on pastures, seed mixes, cover crops, and deep-rooting herbs.

United States Department of Agriculture. *Soils and Men: The 1938 Yearbook of Agriculture.* A wealth of information on soils, tillage, and fertilizer that should be reprinted. This is what the USDA was created to do before its focus shifted toward large-scale agribusiness.

———. *Report and Recommendations on Organic Farming,* 1980. A landmark report, documenting the value and success of commercial organic farmers, as determined by a USDA study team. It called for further research into questions of interest to organic farmers, and has been largely ignored by subsequent administrations.

Waksman, S. *Humus.* New York: John Wiley & Sons, 1948.

————. *Soil Microbiology*. New York: John Wiley & Sons, 1952. The dean of American soil microbiologists. His earlier work on humus has not been surpassed.

Walters, C., and C.J. Fenzau. *An Acres USA Primer*. Raytown, Mo.: Acres USA, 1979. A lesson-by-lesson approach to the techniques of ecological agriculture.

Wistinghausen, et al. *Bio-Dynamic Farming Practice*. Clent, UK: Bio-Dynamic Agriculture Association, 1990. A detailed, thorough text, useful to those seeking practical guidance in applying biodynamic principles on their farms.

Yeomans, P.A. *Water for Every Farm: Yeomans Keyline Plan*. Queensland, Australia: Keyline Designs, 1993. A dynamic approach to arid/dryland farming.

TECHNICAL REFERENCES

The following is a collection of useful technical reference books. Most are ecologically oriented. This is not an exhaustive listing, but a starting point for the serious researcher.

Alexander, M. *Introduction to Soil Microbiology*. New York: Wiley & Co., 1961.

Allen, M. *Ecology of Mycorrhizae*. Cambridge, UK: Cambridge University Press, 1991.

Ankerman, D. and R. Large. *Soil and Plant Analysis*. A & L Agricultural Laboratories, Inc. Undated.

Ardapple-Kindberg, Eric and Beth. *Soil Fertility for Organic Farmers*. Bass, Ariz: Keyline Environmental Management Systems, 1991.

Baker, K. and R. Cook. *Biological Control of Plant Pathogens*. San Francisco: Freeman Co., 1974.

Bartholomew and Clark, eds. *Soil Nitrogen*. Madison, Wisc.: American Society of Agronomy, 1965.

Bear, F.E. *Soils in Relation to Crop Growth*. New York: Reinhold, 1965.

————. *Chemistry of the Soil*. New York: Reinhold, 1967.

Besson, J. M., and H. Vogtmann, eds. *Towards a Sustainable Agriculture*. Verlag Wirz A6, AArau. 1977.

Black, et al. *Methods of Soil Analysis*. Madison, Wisc.: American Society of Agronomy, 1965.

Boeringa, R., ed. *Alternative Methods of Agriculture*. Amsterdam: Elsevier Scientific Publishing, 1980.

Brady, Nyle. *The Nature and Properties of Soils, Tenth Edition*. New York: Macmillan, 1990.

Chaney, D., et al. *Organic Soil Amendments & Fertilizers*. University of California. Division of Agriculture & Natural Resources, 1992.

Davies, B. *Applied Soil Trace Elements*. New York: John Wiley & Sons, 1980.

Dindal, Daniel, ed. *Soil Biology Guide*. New York: John Wiley & Sons, 1990.

Durno, J., I. Moeliono, and R. Prasertcharoensuk. *Sustainable Agriculture for the Lowlands*. Bangkok, Thailand: Southeast Asia Sustainable Agriculture Network, 1992.

Edens, et al. *Sustainable Agriculture and Integrated Farming Systems*. East Lansing, Mich.: Michigan State University Press, 1984.

Foster, R.C., A. Rovira, and T. Cock. *Ultrastructure of the Root-Soil Interface*. St. Paul, Minn.: American Phytopathological Society, 1983.

Golueke, C.G. *Composting: A Study of the Processes and its Principles*. Emmaus, Pa.: Rodale Press, 1972.

Hill, S., and P. Ott, eds. *Basic Techniques in Ecological Farming and the Maintenance of Soil Fertility*. Basel, Switzerland: Berkhauser Verlag, 1982.

Jackson, W.R. *Organic Soil Conditioning: Humic, Fulvic & Microbial Balance*. Evergreen, Colo.: Jackson Research Center, 1993.

Khasawneh, F., et al., eds. *The Role of Phosphorus in Agriculture*. Madison, Wisc.: American Society of Agronomy, 1980.

Killham, Ken. *Soil Ecology*. Cambridge, UK: Cambridge University Press, 1994.

Kilmer, V., et al., eds. *The Role of Potassium in Agriculture*. Madison, Wisc.: American Society of Agronomy, 1968.

Knorr, D. *Sustainable Food Systems*. Westport, Conn.: AVI Publishing Co., 1983.

Lockeretz, W., ed. *Environmentally Sound Agriculture*. New York: Praeger, 1983.

McAllister, J.A. *Practical Guide to Novel Soil Amendments*. Emmaus, Pa.: Rodale Press, 1983.

McLeod, E. *Feed the Soil*. Oak Park, Mich.: McLeod Publishing, 1982.

Merkel, J.A. *Managing Livestock Wastes*. Westport, Conn.: AVI Publishing Co., 1981.

Miller, P.R., et al. *Covercrops for California Agriculture*. University of California Division of Agriculture & Natural Resources, 1989.

Mulongoy and Merckx, eds. *Soil Organic Matter Dynamics & Sustainability of Tropical Agriculture*. New York: John Wiley & Sons, 1993.

National Research Council. *Sustainable Agriculture & the Environment in the Humid Tropics*. Washington, D.C.: National Academy Press, 1993.

———. *Alternative Agriculture*. Washington, D.C.: National Academy Press, 1989.

Pfeiffer, E. *Compost Manufacturer's Manual*. Spring Valley, N.Y.: Anthrosophic Press, 1950.

———. *Sensitive Crystallization Processes*. Spring Valley, N.Y.: Anthroposophic Press, 1936.

Pfleger and Linderman, Eds. *Mycorrhizae & Plant Health*. St. Paul, Minn.: American Phytopathological Society, 1994.

Raven, P.H., R.F. Evert, and S.E. Eichhorn. *Biology of Plants*. New York: Worth Publishers, 1992.

Russell, D. *Soil Conditions and Plant Growth*. New York: John Wiley & Sons, 1973.

Sanchez, Pedro. *Properties & Management of Soils in the Tropics*. New York: John Wiley and Sons, 1976.

Engelstad, O.F., ed. *Nutrient Mobility in Soils: Accumulation & Losses*, Special Publication No. 4. Madison, Wisc.: Soil Science Society of America, 1970.

Stonehouse, B. *Biological Husbandry*. London: Butterworths, 1981.

Tisdale, Nelson, Beaton and Havlin. *Soil Fertility & Fertilizers*, Fifth edition. New York: Macmillan Publishing Co, 1993.

Van Wambeke, Armand. *Soils of the Tropics: Properties & Appraisal*. New York: McGraw-Hill, 1992.

Walsh, L., and J. Beaton. *Soil Testing and Plant Analysis*. Madison, Wisc.: Soil Science Society of America, 1973.

Weaver, R. *Plant Growth Substances in Agriculture*. San Francisco, Calif.: Freeman, 1972.

INDEX

ABOUT THE AUTHORS

GRACE GERSHUNY has been active in alternative agriculture for over twenty years, as an organic farmer, organizer, author, and educator. She is on the faculty of the Institute for Social Ecology and Goddard College, Plainfield, Vermont, and for many years was closely associated with the Northeast Organic Farming Association (NOFA). Ms. Gershuny gained wide recognition as editor of *Organic Farmer: The Digest of Sustainable Agriculture*, published from 1990 to 1994. She is the author of *Start with the Soil* and the co-author of *The Rodale Book of Composting*.

Ms. Gershuny has worked in every aspect of organic certification program development and management, and has served on the staff of the U.S. Department of Agriculture's National Organic Program since 1994. She lives in northeastern Vermont with her husband and daughter.

JOE SMILLIE is the senior vice president of Quality Assurance International, one of the leading organic certification agencies in the world. He is a founding member and past-president of the Organic Trade Association (OTA), which represents the entire spectrum of the organic industry. He is currently the chair of OTA's International Relations committee, and has been instrumental in developing organic certification systems in North America.

Prior to joining QAI, he worked for many years as an independent certification inspector. He is a founding member of the

Independent Organic Inspectors Association (IOIA) and the International Inspectors Group(IIG). As an inspector, consultant, and certification agency representative, Smillie has worked with organic farmers and processors around the world.

Smillie has also co-authored *The Orchard Almanac: A Seasonal Guide to Healthy Fruit Trees*, and *Rodale's Chemical-Free Yard and Garden*. Before coming to the United Sates, he homesteaded with his family on an organic farm in Quebec. The Smillie/Boyer family currently resides in Richmond, Vermont.

The authors also collaborated on drafting the first edition of the *Guidelines for the Organic Industry* for the Organic Trade Association in 1986.

Chelsea Green Publishing is committed to preserving ancient forests and natural resources. We elected to print this title on 30-percent postconsumer recycled paper, processed chlorine-free. As a result, for this printing, we have saved:

2 Trees (40' tall and 6-8" diameter)
1 Million BTUs of Total Energy
193 Pounds of Greenhouse Gases
1,049 Gallons of Wastewater
70 Pounds of Solid Waste

Chelsea Green Publishing made this paper choice because we and our printer, Thomson-Shore, Inc., are members of the Green Press Initiative, a nonprofit program dedicated to supporting authors, publishers, and suppliers in their efforts to reduce their use of fiber obtained from endangered forests. For more information, visit: www.greenpressinitiative.org.

Environmental impact estimates were made using the Environmental Defense Paper Calculator.
For more information visit: www.papercalculator.org.